monologues
for men

He Speaks

nusa '06

He Speaks

monologues for men

compiled and edited by David Ferry

Playwrights Canada Press
Toronto • Canada

PLAYWRIGHTS CANADA PRESS
The Canadian Drama Publisher
215 Spadina Ave., Suite 230, Toronto, Ontario, Canada, M5T 2C7
phone 416.703.0013 fax 416.408.3402
orders@playwrightscanada.com • www.playwrightscanada.com

The publisher acknowledges the support of the Canadian taxpayers through the Government of Canada Book Publishing Industry Development Program, the Canada Council for the Arts, the Ontario Arts Council, and the Ontario Media Development Corporation.

Front cover collage by Nusa Prijatelj
Production Editing/Cover Design by JLArt

LIBRARY AND ARCHIVES CANADA CATALOGUING IN PUBLICATION
Ferry, David
He speaks : monologues for men / compiled and edited by David Ferry.

Includes index.
ISBN 978-0-88754-856-7

1. Monologues, Canadian (English) 2. Men--Drama. I. Title.

PS8309.M6H4 2006   C812'.045089286   C2006-905092-9

First edition: October 2006.
Second printing: February 2009.
Printed and bound by Hignell Book Printing at Winnipeg, Canada.

The publisher thanks the following publishers and authors for the use of the excerpt from the following:

Talonbooks

Consecrated Ground, George Boyd
Salt-Water Moon, David French
The Weekend Healer,
  Bryden MacDonald
alterNatives, Drew Hayden Taylor
Hosanna, Michel Tremblay
For the Pleasure of Seeing Her Again,
  Michel Tremblay
Adult Entertainment, George F. Walker
Risk Everything, George F. Walker
Criminal Genius, George F. Walker
Zastrozzi: The Master of Discipline,
  George F. Walker
Theatre of the Film Noir, George F.
  Walker

NeWest Press

Snake in Fridge, Brad Fraser

House of Anansi Press

Of the Fields, Lately..., David French

Scirocco Drama

Atlantis, Maureen Hunter
Blood, Tom Walmsley
cherry docs, David Gow

Leméac Éditeur

Alphonse, Wajdi Mouawad
Wedding Day at the Cro-Magnons',
  Wajdi Mouawad
Stone and Ashes, Daniel Danis

Red Deer Press

Two Words for Snow, Richard Sanger

Fifth House Publishing

Toronto at Dreamer's Rock, Drew
  Hayden Taylor

Dundurn Press

Fathers and Sons, Don Hannah

Exile Editions

Children, Lawrence Jeffery

Table of Contents

David Ferry is a director, dramaturge, actor and teacher. He is the current Consulting Artistic Director of Resurgence Theatre Company and the York Shakespeare Festival. David was Artistic Director of Bluewater Summer Playhouse in Kincardine, Ontario from 1998-2002.

David won the 2006 Dora Mavor Moore award for Best Direction for *The Last Days of Judas Iscariot* (also Best Production Dora) and was invited to the 2006 Festival Intercity in Florence, Italy where he directed Brendan Gall's *Alias Godot* in Italian. As a dramaturge, David has worked with a number of writers including Florence Gibson, Brendan Gall, Fides Krucker, Kelly McIntosh, Paul Ledoux, David Smyth, John Roby, James Reaney, Robert Priest, Drew Hayden Taylor, and Tom Walmsley.

David has worked as an actor at the Stratford Festival and in most theatres across the country as well as on and off Broadway in New York. He works as frequently in film, television, and radio as he does on stage, and has been nominated for or won acting awards such as the Dora Mavor Moore, Genie, Gemini, and Nellie.

David has taught acting at theatre schools across Canada, and has published an internationally recognized CD collection of Canadian dialects for the actor ("Canadian, Eh?").

David has served on the executives of CAEA, ACTRA and is currently a Governor of Actra Fraternal Benefit Society.

David was a graduate of the National Theatre School of Canada (1973) and has his Master of Fine Arts in Theatre Directing (MFA) from the University of Victoria (2003), where he focused on the work of James Reaney.

Introduction

As early as 1960 playwright and poet James Reaney preached for

> "...seasons of plays by Canadians, [which should be done in] bare
> long room[s] above [stores], probably infested with Odd Fellows or
> Orangemen on easily avoidable nights. Nobody should have any
> truck with that grand Bugaboo—Lighting. Five two hundred
> Mazda watters always turned on will do for any play that lights its
> own way, as a play should." [1]

Ten years after Reaney's recipe for an indigenous Canadian Theatre, theatre
artists were doing just that from St. John's (the Longshoremen's Protective
Union Hall) to Montreal (Old Stock Exchange) to Toronto (the parking
Garage at Rochdale Collage; an old candle factory on Dupont Street; an old
gasworks on Berkeley Street) to Winnipeg (Grain Exchange Building) to
Vancouver (Grandview Methodist Church).

When I started my studies at the National Theatre School (NTS) in 1970
only a minority of the established regional theatres in Canada were
doing indigenous plays in their seasons (a nationalist might be excused for
considering them token productions). However the "alternative" theatre
movement of the late sixties and early seventies was mostly focused on
Canadian playwrights or (in the case of the collective companies) Canadian
stories. These theatres evolved during a time of increasing Canadian
nationalism in the post-Centennial years and attracted loyal audiences
hungry for plays about our own culture. The influence of the alternative
theatres on the mainstream in terms of programming Canadian plays and
stories was considerable (as well as on the policies of the Canada Council and
various provincial arts councils).

As a young actor graduating from the NTS in this era it was difficult to
find audition pieces from the Canadian Canon. Certainly I was fortunate
enough to be involved in the birth of a lot of new plays, and monologues that
I, and others of my generation, had spoken in premiere productions soon
began to turn up in the audition rooms across the country. But still those
great monologues were limited and auditors saw a *lot* of duplication.

Today we have grown so far from those early post-Centennial days it has
been actually impossible to review all the plays that are out there when I was

looking for material for this book. When I helped edit *You're Making a Scene* for Playwright's Canada Press in 1993, the list of plays I read was long, but nothing like the list I surveyed for this collection. It's interesting that only eight of the authors featured in *You're Making a Scene* are represented here among the sixty-four playwrights included in *He Speaks*. The reason is not that the other playwrights featured in *You're Making a Scene* are no longer relevant or interesting, it's just that there is so much fine work out there that we have an embarrassment of riches to choose from.

One of the more exciting developments in the progress of our playwrights over the last thirteen years is in the breadth of the voices speaking out in Canadian theatres. While we certainly need to see more authors from non-Eurocentric cultural backgrounds on our stages, the growth of writers from AfriCanadian, Asian (Chinese, Japanese, Malaysian) Canadian, Middle Eastern Canadian, Indo and Pakistani Canadian cultural backgrounds has been considerable. As well we have seen the increased growth of First Nations writing for the theatre. Authors that self identify as gay or lesbian have found a great deal more stage time in Canada, and the feminist playwriting movement has given birth to whole new generations of young women writers. Also, of late, thankfully, political theatre is making a comeback. As well, a great many young playwrights are now happily staying at home to ply their trade instead of automatically heading off to larger centres. Newfoundland has developed one of the most vibrant artistic communities in the country. Calgary is probably the most vibrant hotspot of Canadian theatre activity. In those places, as well as elsewhere, writers have multiple stages or companies to feature their work and these writers all seem to share a desire to author works reflective of not just local concerns but of international issues.

There are many authors included in *He Speaks* who have an extraordinary body of work behind them. George Walker, Judith Thompson, Jason Sherman, Daniel MacIvor, just to name a few, all offer so many tempting pieces to choose from. There are also writers who are relatively new on the scene and have fresh viewpoints for us to consider. The startling voices of Joseph Pierre, Gina Wilkinson, Anton Piatigorsky and Kristen Thomson all come to mind. What strikes me in re-reading the entries in *He Speaks* is the beautiful use of language and imagery on display. From Michael Ondaatje's searing description of drunk rats in *The Collected Works of Billy the Kid: Left Handed Poems* to David Gow's percussive use of monosyllabic words and short abbreviated sentences in Mike's monologue from *cherry docs* to Wajdi Mouawad's violent imagistic prose in contrast to his delicate Haiku like poetry in *Wedding Day at the Cro-Magnons'* to Mieko Ouchi's elegant and elegiac verbal painting of a woman as she morphs into a statue in *The Red Priest (Eight Ways to Say Goodbye)* to Kent Stetson's poetic lyricism in describing a farmer's world in *Horse High, Bull Strong, Pig Tight* to Bryden MacDonald's almost pop lyric directness and rhythm in expressing a teen's alienation in *The Weekend Healer* you will find a cornucopia of well crafted writing that is a joy to read and speak. Also abundant is writing infused with humour, irony, grief, longing, regret, desire, mystery, anger, jealousy, pain, happiness and all the other essential ingredients of good theatre. *He Speaks* reveals a group of authors possessed with a burning desire to shed light on the human condition.

When wondering how to order the selections in *He Speaks* I agonized over various thematic, cultural and regional delineations for the monologues. One of the realizations I came to is that we no longer need (if we ever did) to ghettoize our writers. Why should one author be noted as AfriCanadian and another as First Nations while those without designation are assumed to be the norm (i.e. the great white Canuck)? Similarly I could get into real hot water by limiting an author by stipulating "place."

In seeking thematic links for the monologues of *He Speaks* I looked to and greatly admired the superb collection and their thematic linking by Judith Thompson in *He Speaks'* wonderful sister collection *She Speaks* (Playwrights Canada Press). I looked at the imaginative co-opting that an actor must perform when assimilating a character's needs and desires for thematic inspiration; "I remember"; "I desire"; "I hate"; "I wish"; "I believe", etc., but in the end I found so many different kinds of monologues, each one, like the author, unique in interior theme and motif. As hard as I tried I just couldn't find a comfortable thematic breakdown of the *He Speaks* monologues I had chosen. I finally decided that I didn't want to limit the author to my perceived themes. I think the monologues tell ninety-four different stories and they each "light their own way," as James Reaney says, "as a play [monologue] should."

When directing actors (student or professional) I will always ask these questions: what light do you want to shed on the human condition? Why are you saying these things here and now? It seems to me that if an actor isn't possessed of his/her own personal passion to shed light with the author's words, then he/she may as well stay home. In seeking ways to help actors personalize the author's words I often attempt to find a common language with the actor so they may take ownership of the language. I lean towards the use of active verbs in this common language, and one of my favourite questions is "what are you fighting for?" This question immediately puts the actor in the driver's seat. It propels the actor forward as if into a life or death struggle. If the answer to this question is specific and high stakes, then the result is much more likely to engage us passionately and the author's words are much more likely to become our own. Then we might just be in a place where we too can shed light.

If you are looking at these monologues with an eye to finding an audition piece I advise you to find something that engages your passion, your humour, your sense of justice, something you can care about. Pick something that you can really fight for, and please, look for the script (I have tried to indicate sources for every play represented) and read the whole play before you tackle the monologue. The monologue is like the tip of one of those seasonal icebergs that float so majestically down the Newfoundland coastline. They catch one's breath, but underneath lies the other nine tenths of the beast, an ice-blue bedrock, glowing as if with an inner light.

I came across a beautiful Inuit Song as I started to write this introduction, a friend had sent it to me via email. It reminded me in a profound way of what all the writers do in these monologues, and it reminded me too of Reaney's wonderful vision for a Canadian Theatre.

Old Inuit Song[2]

I think over again my small adventures.
My Fears,
Those small ones that seemed so big,
For all the vital things
I had to get and to reach.

And yet there is only one great thing,
The only thing,
To live to see the great day that dawns
And the light that fills the world.

Each author represented here does what the Inuit hunter/shaman/poet (quite possibly the extraordinary Kibkarjuk Orpingalik) singing this song does. She/he looks closely at the small adventures of each human and talks about fears that often seem so large as to overwhelm us or they reach inside to seek the vital things they need to express. Sometimes they will talk about horror, sometimes about love. Sometimes the love they examine is also the horror they expose. They will look at memories and sort them or they will rage at the machine. They will seek to find their identity in the shifting sands of an ever-changing universe. They will throw up images of stark beauty or complex ugliness; propose maxims with deep moral implications or question slippery ethical standards; they will juxtapose the ludicrous with the divine and they will mock, glorify, penetrate or expose just about everything in society. All these will our authors do to discover the only "one great thing"— the story. The story is the universe for each author, and the objective with each story surely is to in some way shed light. At times a writer is fortunate enough, not only to shed light, but also to shed a light that fills the world of the viewer or reader. With each writer I read in compiling this collection (hundreds of selections/submissions read) I looked for some kind of light. How happy was my search in that I found so much light. I hope you enjoy these selections as much as I do. I hope they light up your life as they have mine.

David Ferry
May 2006

Notes

1 Reaney, James. Editorial. *Alphabet: A semiannual devoted to the Iconography of the Imagination* (London, Ontario: 1960) 1. 1.

2 For a fine collection of Inuit Poems see John Robert Colombo's *The Poems of the Inuit*, (Canada: Oberon Press 1981). In that book there is a version of this poem called *Little Song* (104). Danish explorer Knud Rasmussen linked this version of the traditional song to the Copper Inuits: "a little nameless Eskimo song from the Kitlinguharmiut." (Colombo, John Robert. Notes, *The Poems of the Inuit*, p113.) There is a also a version of this song in Fred Bruemmer's *Seasons of the Eskimo* (Toronto ON: McClelland and Stewart, 1971).

from

For the Pleasure of Seeing Her Again
by Michel Tremblay
translated by Linda Gaboriau

Premiered at the Centaur Theatre Company, Montreal, 1998, directed by
Gordon McCall. Script available from Talonbooks.

• • •

NARRATOR

Tonight, no one will rage and cry: "My kingdom for a horse!" No ghost will
come to haunt the battlements of a castle in the kingdom of Denmark
where, apparently, something is rotten. Nor will anyone wring her hands
and murmur: "Leave, I do not despise you." Three still young women will
not retreat of a dacha, whispering the name of Moscow, their beloved, their
lost hope. No sister will await the return of her brother to avenge the death
of their father, no son will be forced to avenge an affront to his father, no
mother will kill her three children to take revenge on their father. And no
husband will see his doll-like wife leave him out of contempt. No one will
turn into a rhinoceros. Maids will not plot to assassinate their mistress,
after denouncing her lover and having him jailed. No one will fret about
"the rain in Spain!" No one will emerge from a garbage pail to tell an
absurd story. Italian families will not leave for the seashore. No soldier
will return from World War II and bang on his father's bedroom door,
protesting the presence of a new wife in his mother's bed. No evanescent
blonde will drown. No Spanish nobleman will seduce a thousand and three
women, nor will an entire family of Spanish women writhe beneath the
heel of the fierce Bernarda Alba. You won't see a brute of a man rip his
sweat-drenched T-shirt, shouting: "Stella! Stella!" and his sister-in-law will
not be doomed the minute she steps off the streetcar named Desire. Nor
will you see a stepmother pine away for her new husband's youngest son.
The plague will not descend on the city of Thebes, and the Trojan War will
not take place. No king will be betrayed by his ungrateful daughters. There
will be no duels, no poisonings, no wracking coughs. No one will die, or
if someone must die, it will become a comic scene. No, there will be none
of the usual theatrics. What you will see tonight is a very simple woman,
a woman who will simply talk.... I almost said, about her life, but the lives

of others will be just as important: her husband, her sons, her relatives and neighbours. Perhaps you will recognize her. You've often run into her at the theatre, in the audience and on stage, you've met her in life, she's one of you. She was born, it's true, during a specific era in this country and lived her life in a city that resembles this city, but, I am convinced, she is everywhere. She is universal. She is Rodrigue's aunt, Electra's cousin, Ivanov's sister, Caligula's stepmother, Mistress Quickly's little niece, the mother of Ham or of Clov, or perhaps both. And when she speaks in her own words, people who speak differently will understand her, in their own words. She has existed throughout the ages and in every culture. She always has been present and always will be. I wanted the pleasure of seeing her again. The pleasure of hearing her. So she could make me laugh and cry. One more time, if I may. *(He looks towards the wings.)* Aha, I hear her coming. Get ready, she'll talk a blue streak, because words have always been her most effective weapon. *(He smiles.)* As they say in the classics: "Hark, she cometh this way!"

from

Sled
by Judith Thompson

Premiered at the Tarragon Theatre, Toronto, 1997, directed by Duncan McIntosh. Script available from Playwrights Canada Press.

• • •

JACK confesses his infidelity to his wife.

JACK

Annie? You in the bath? You enjoy your bath, I won't bother you. I know how much you love your long bath. I was thinking about what you were talking about, my temper. Like my… anger. The local punks callin' me "*Diablo.*" What I did to those kids tonight and that thing with Pochinshky on Eglinton. I was thinking—I have to tell you something I haven't told you yet.

Remember, we ran into that—Jemma? The legal secretary from Brantford, blonde with the moussed hair—in February. Remember? At Yorkdale Mall? And remember how uncomfortable you said you felt? The way she looked at you? You said you thought there was something…

I used to… get very pissed at Jemma.

Sometimes I think it was because she was blonde. And she was so big breasted. I, like, I wanted to own her. I would leave you at home reading in your nightgown, tellin' you I had to work all night and I would drive to Brantford to see Jemma, to have sex with her four, five times every which way I did things to her that… and then I would drive home and slide into bed next to you and we would talk that sweet night talk and you were so trusting—I was an animal. I was out of control. I still don't get it. I don't get why it happened. I didn't tell you before because I was afraid you wouldn't forgive me; maybe you won't forgive me, maybe you'll get outta the bath and say you want a separation, I wouldn't blame you. But I love you so much I wanted to tell you the whole truth. I was good as golden right up till I was nine. You know? The perfect kid. I would give my dad the paper, ask him if he wanted a beer, go get it for him, help my mama with the table, change my baby sister. Sundays, I would put on the little suit, and we'd go to church. My sister and I would get under a blanket on the couch and watch cartoons all morning. I'd talk French with my gramma, sing songs with her; I played every sport goin', hockey, baseball, soccer, everything. I slept with my football. And then this kid, at school, he started to pick on me. Take off my hat in winter, throw it around. Say I was cheating in ball hockey. I never cheated. But he was a grade older, bigger, and said I couldn't play ball hockey. And I would sit there, on the side, and hope to be asked.

It was around then, I got—angry at home. I put holes in the walls with my fists. I wouldn't talk French wouldn't eat French, if my mother put tourtière and sugar pie on the table I would throw 'em on the floor, "You stupid bitch, I want a hamburger and a fuckin' popsicle not this frog shit, not this…" I never kissed a woman till you, Annie. I would turn away. I would say, I'm not one for kissing. Because kissing meant… I don't know. Being there. Goin' inside like an underwater cave with someone, swimmin' in, hand in hand, with this person, and so much so much could go wrong. You're not the first woman I slept with, as you know, and maybe not the last, as you also know, but you are the first, and the last woman I will ever kiss.

Annie?

from

The Domino Heart
by Matthew Edison

Premiered at the Tarragon Theatre, Toronto, co-produced by Jack in the Black Theatre, 2003, directed by Michael Kessler. Script available from Playwrights Canada Press.

• • •

> *REVEREND MORTIMER WRIGHT is awaiting a heart transplant operation which will take place in a little over an hour. He has just been reminded of a childhood friend who committed suicide when he was a teenager.*

MORT

Live as if you're dying because you are.

In a few hours I'm going to have a new heart. The old one's given out. I like to think it's because I overused it.

It's a waiting game now while they "harvest the organ." They don't often call it a heart here in the transplant world, it's "the organ." Nancy, the organist at St. Paul's said, "Just make sure this one's in tune and try to keep the pipes clean." She likes to remonstrate with me for the years I consumed Bertie's smoked meat sandwiches without heeding a single of her warnings. "The heart has its own plans," I tell her, "it follows naught but itself." As if I were quoting someone else.

It's very controversial back home. Shouldn't a man of the cloth respect the fate God has handed him? After all, isn't this what I've been waiting for? Heaven and eternal paradise await me on the other side. I don't know about that. I have some questions to be perfectly honest about it but I like my job, I like raising people's spirits, as it were. I'm good at it and I get a lot of joy out of it. Nancy likes to tease me. She said, "Geez, Mortimer, what do you wanna hang around here for? You've had nearly seventy good years with that heart of yours." I said, "I know, but I was given a lifetime guarantee." And she said, "No, Mort, no one is given that."

Beat.

It's possible that my body, this church, may not accept the gift of this new *organ* so… if it's not to be, heaven and eternal paradise would be a nice runner-up.

We'll see. My prayer remains the same: for *harmony*.

from   ✓

I Am Yours
by Judith Thompson

Premiered at the Tarragon Theatre, Toronto, 1987, directed by Derek
Goldby. Script available from Playwrights Canada Press.

• • •

> *MACK describes the discovery of a bee's nest in his childhood
> home.*

MACK

When I was nine I was stung by a thousand bees; one hundred fifty-seven
stingers in my nine-year-old body, I was on a respirator for three days. I can
still feel it, hear it. My mother, Joy, was a cleaning fanatic, obsessed; every
time you opened our front door, you'd hear *vroooooom*, she vacuumed
twice a day, you'd almost pass out from the fumes of the bleach and the
Pine-Sol. I always slipped on the over-waxed floor. She'd have done three
or four loads of laundry before she woke up my sister and me at seven; she
washed the kitchen floor with straight bleach every day.

I remember the first, the first bee, I was about nine and I was having a glass
of milk after my soccer game, in the kitchen, she was standing over me
waiting to clean it, and there was this buzzing. *Bzzzzzzzz bzzzzzz*, my
mother looked around, *bzzzzzz*, and then it stung her, on the hand. Her
hand swelled up badly, she ran the cold water. *Bzzzzz*, I spotted another, by
the fridge, and then another on the ceiling, she was frantic. We opened the
pantry and although everything was, like, perfectly stored and packaged
there were four or five or six of these bees buzzing around. One of them
came after me, it actually chased me. I ran to the third floor, it chased me
all through the house and then stung me hard on the lip, it hurt so much.
My mother, she stood in the pantry like a cat, watching the walls, trying
to figure out where they were coming from. I'm watching TV, suddenly
wham bash, I run to the pantry and there is my mother, my clean mother
smashing in the pantry wall with my baseball bat. Down came the plaster,
filling the air with dust, and then the lath, and then she's tearing away the
pink insulation, sobbing and choking, and I'm trying to see through all this
dust. The buzzing sound was deafening like the bass of an electric guitar

turned way up, *bzzzzzzzz*, and there it was... huge, majestic, a shimmering tower of bees, a six-foot honeycomb, dripping, behind our wall, hundreds, no thousands of bees swarming around it protecting their queen, all for the queen, and they swarmed us, stung us, over and over, the honey poured thick from the hive, into our pantry, into our house, unstoppable over bleached linoleum floor and into the hall, seeped in the carpet.... And since that time I have thought, I have known that there is something deadly, yes, but I don't know really... glorious behind every wall. Deirdre. Her fear of things behind walls? Her eyes?

from

Of the Fields, Lately...
by David French

Premiered at the Tarragon Theatre, Toronto, 1973, directed by Bill Glassco. Script available from House of Anansi Press.

• • •

> *WIFF is trying to make Mary understand why he was drunk at the Oakwood Hotel and not at the hospital the night his wife died.*

WIFF

I had my first whiskey, and no sooner had I drunk it than somet'ing came back to me so clear… *(He sits.)* The first time Dot and me ever met. T'irty-five years ago. Me on my way down to the coal shed to unload the steamer, her on her way to the church to light the fire. How it all came back, suddenly sitting at that table. That dark road, the stars still out, and me with my flashlight and lunchpail, no older than Ben. And who comes tripping along the road towards me, but Dot, the beam of her flashlight bouncing and swinging. I puts the light in her young face, and for a moment I don't recognize her, she's blossomed out that much in the time I was away in Boston…. "Is that you, Dot Snow?" And she laughs. I'd forgot how gentle laughter could be. "Is that you, Wiff Roach?" Well, duckie, I never made it to the coal shed that morning. No, by God, I never. And my father couldn't have dragged me, had he kicked my ass all the way with his biggest boots. I walked her up the road, instead, and we sat in her family pew till the sun come up. Two months later we was married. You remembers, Mary. You was the bridesmaid. *(slight pause—WIFF stands)* So that's how come I never made it to the hospital yesterday. I had another whiskey to ease the pain I was feeling, and a t'ird because the second never helped…. So if you wants to hurt me, Mary, you go right ahead, my dear, but you're too late… and not'ing you can ever say or do will make me feel worse than knowing what Dot and me once had and what it come to in the end, without either one of us ever knowing why… *(He sits again.)* And that's why I want her buried in her wedding dress, if you must know, in spite of what she said at the last. What she wanted in those days is just as real to me as what she wanted yesterday. Nor do it have the same sadness, Mary, not the same sadness at all...

from

Here Lies Henry
by Daniel MacIvor and Daniel Brooks

Premiered at the Six Stages Festival at Buddies in Bad Times Theatre, Toronto, 1995, directed and dramaturged by Daniel Brooks. Script available from Playwrights Canada Press.

• • •

HENRY finally tells the truth.

HENRY

And so, say you die

...and I know that's a scary thing but only because you don't know what happens, so I'm going to tell you.

When you die you float up to the ceiling and then you hit the ceiling and when you hit the ceiling you open your eyes and you find yourself in a white room in a kind of uncomfortable chair. And every time you close your eyes your life plays itself out from the beginning, in real time. And so you decide to close your eyes and watch. And then when your life is over a woman comes into the room, she's your maternal grandmother when she was eighteen years old and you don't really recognize her because you didn't know her then. And she takes you by the arm and leads you out of the room, through a wheat field, across a beach and over what looks like it might be the surface of the moon, to a room that is filled with photographs of every person whose eyes ever met yours. And she tells you a little bit about each of them. And then you feel tired so she leads you to an attic that is filled with mattresses from every bed you have ever slept in, and in the centre of the room is the mattress from the bed in which you were conceived, and she tells you to lie down there, and you do, and you fall into a deep and restful sleep. And then you are woken up by the person you always felt you should have spent your life with but didn't. And then you get to spend a month together. And at the end of the month your dad comes to pick you up. And he drives you through every storm you ever slept through to a room with a table in it and three chairs. And he leaves you there standing before the table and three people enter the room: the first person you kissed, the first person you cursed, and the first person you saw dead. And they explain many many things to you, that you don't understand. And then they let you go through your best friend's closet and wear all your favourite stuff. And then they tell you you must enter a room filled with people and you must tell these people something they don't already know.

And before you can ask why
you find yourself in a room full of people.
People you know,
people you don't know,
people you love,
people you wished loved you,
strangers…
mostly strangers…
and you try to tell these people something that they don't already know.

And then you realize that that is quite impossible. Because how can I tell you what you don't know when I don't even know what I know.

Well, I guess I know a few things.

from

The Darling Family
by Linda Griffiths

Premiered at Theatre Passe Muraille, Toronto, 1991, directed by the company. Script available from Playwrights Canada Press.

• • •

HE and SHE are a new young couple around town. SHE gets pregnant after a relationship of three months (or, according to him, two-and-a-half). The situation challenges everything they know and don't know. There is no set, lighting cues or sound cues. Only two actors speaking their thoughts, ravishing their dreams, being polite, screaming in pain and when in doubt, going to the movies. They almost never fight, they almost never love.

HE

Once I asked my mother's friend, "Do you know where my father is?" I was four years old. And they told him and made him visit me. I was insane with joy. But he couldn't look at me. He sat around with the friends who brought him and played cards. I kept running into the kitchen to look at him. He'd turn around and go, "Hi there." He tried to talk to me but he couldn't. Couldn't look and couldn't talk. Just an introverted kind of person with his own problems, how could he relate to me? I went into the bedroom and bent over by the bed, laid my head down on the covers. I stayed there till they found me and made me throw darts at a board. Somewhere in all that time, he left. Rock and roll helped. Music helped. I was the guy drinking beer with the bands backstage because I likened their lyrics to Proust. My head is full of trivia about who played bass with The Cramps and why Johnny Rotton learned to play piano. But how long is a generation in that world? Two years. Because in two years you neither know nor truly care what bands are starting out anymore. It helped, but it's a trap if you're not in the band. You're either in the band or out of the band.

from

alterNatives
by Drew Hayden Taylor

Premiered at the Bluewater Summer Playhouse, Kincardine, 1999, directed by David Ferry. Script available from Talonbooks.

• • •

About the dinner party from hell where politically active Native people do battle over a moose roast with politically correct non-Natives.

ANGEL

Thanks. Okay, picture it. There's this Native astronaut and he's cruising at the edge of the solar system in his space ship. And he's in a bad mood because back on Earth everybody is celebrating. The biggest party since... whenever, because the very last land claim has finally been settled. You gotta understand, this is about a hundred years into the future. It'll take about that long. So everyone on every Reserve is partying it up while this poor guy is stuck alone somewhere out past Pluto. He picks something funny up on his scanners and goes to investigate. As he approaches the far rim of the solar system, in uncharted territory, he discovers a big space... thing. It's covered in flashing lights, and is just hovering out there, evidently trying to attract attention. The astronaut's sensors are going nuts. The thing wants to be understood but his scanners can't make heads or tails out of its communications. But gradually, the thing understands that the astronaut speaks English and in translation the thing begins to spell out a message. So this Native astronaut reads the very first message from an alien civilization. This big flashing thing suddenly says, in English, "For Sale." You get it, it's a huge interstellar billboard. Evidently the solar system is up for sale. The astronaut stares at it in disbelief. Then suddenly the sign slowly begins to change. It now says "Sold." Somebody's just bought the solar system. The Native astronaut mutters to himself "Not again." The end.

from

El Paso
by Michael A. Miller

Premiered at Factory Theatre, Toronto, 2002, directed by Philip Akin. Script available from the playwright at mmille0282@rogers.com.

• • •

> *PAPA SPILLER is a Black man in his early eighties. An ailing*
> *tyrant if you will. At this juncture PAPA has just found out*
> *that his house is being demolished by the city to make room*
> *for a highway. He has also found out that his eldest daughter*
> *withheld this information from him for her own gain.*

PAPA

They are ripping down my house for a highway. Like it was nothing. I built this house to last. As a refuge from the cruel world outside those four brick walls. You don't know what it took to get a house like that. The son of slaves. I grew up in reconstruction. After the hell of slavery, reconstruction was the heaven on earth we had been singing about. Families could stay together. Homes could be built. Businesses could be owned. We were allowed to be human. For once time was on our side and boy we made the most of it. But the world can turn on a dime. There were those who didn't like to see that we were human. That we could run the same race and run twice as fast and win just sometimes. They wanted to turn back the clock. So Jim Crow came a calling. It wasn't nothing but slavery dressed up in different clothes. And when we, who knew slaves, and had been slaves, had smelled the blood of it, and we tried to fight back, to keep moving this country forward, we were slaughtered. Riots. Lynchings. Terror. No place to just be human. To have a house free from care. I got the hell out of East Texas and moved west. El Paso was heaven. Bad soil so you never had to bend your back working some field for nothing. Mexico at your back in case you needed to run, and heat so fierce this town was just to pass through but not to stay put. I got a job on the trains and worked for forty years cooking. I beat Jim Crow at his own game. Thrived during the nightmare and turned it into a dream. I had a house where I could raise my children in peace and my wife never had to leave to go work in some white lady's kitchen. I was a man. Black flesh, red blood, white bones, green money and brick walls. I saw my dreams rise from the sand and now I have to see it turn to dust. My house is being ripped down and there is nobody here to mourn its passing. Many a Negro passed my house and pointed up and said "See that big house right over there? William Spiller lives there. He's got the biggest house of any Negro within the county line…" I had the biggest house of any… I'm alive and already feel forgotten. My house is going to dust.

from

This Night the Kapo
by Robert Majzels

Premiered at the Berkeley Street Theatre, Toronto, produced by TEATRON, 2004, directed by Ari Weisberg. Script available from Playwrights Canada Press.

• • •

BENNY is 40 years old, Jewish, manager of a clothing factory. BENNY and his younger brother David are reunited after several years apart. It's late at night. They are in their old family home which, following the death of their father, is now BENNY's. BENNY has just admitted that his wife has recently left him.

BENNY

Who says there's a reason? Where is it written there has to be a reason for everything? Maybe she got tired of the house; it was too big. Maybe she didn't like the black Cadillac; she wanted a pink one. She's allergic to mink. Maybe it was too hard, sitting around the house watching TV, while I busted my ass down at the shop. How the hell should I know? Ungrateful bitch. I never made her work a day in her life. She didn't have to lift a goddamn finger. Even when I was working for Steiner at the beginning, and Papa got sick. It was touch and go there for a while. But did I drag her into it? No sir, not Benny. Never made her lift a finger. Good old Benny kept her nice and comfortable and out of all the drek. Good old Benny. Benny the shmuck.

What? A message? That's a good one. Sure, she left a message. Trouble is she left too many messages. She left them all over the house. Everywhere. Little fucking messages popping up all over the place. The first night, I went to the fridge, there's a note, taped inside the door: Benny, clean out every month. That's it: clean out every month. Nothing else. So, I go to the cupboard for something to eat. And there's a grocery list taped on the edge of the shelf. All neatly printed and divided up in sections. "Dairy products," and underneath: "one carton of milk, one pound semi-salted butter, seven yogourts"—I like to have a yogourt every night around the time the news comes on—so she's got "seven yogourts"—and, in brackets, the brand and everything: "Astro, light, the blue tops." And that's not all: under that, she puts exactly where I can find the dairy counter in the grocery store: "last aisle in the back." She laid it all out for me, where to find it, and all the right quantities, for one person. And special advice, like, "don't go Thursday night; it's too crowded, nor Friday; there's nothing left." And that's it. In the breadbox, I found the address of the baker where she buys the black bread I like. At first I thought it was a good sign: I figured she was worried about me, how I'd make out without her. But then, it got weird. On the inside of the toilet lid: "wash this with Mr. Clean twice a week." Pinned to my pillow, right in my bed: "Change the sheets every week." It was like a minefield in here: messages, like booby traps, springing up at me everywhere I looked. On the bathroom mirror, in red lipstick: "clean your bath after you use it." Like she went nuts. I didn't know what to do. At first, I tried to follow the messages, you know, do what they said. But it was crazy, I was going around in circles. I didn't have the time. I felt like an idiot. Reading little notes and following her orders like some kind of zombie. The thing was, I couldn't bring myself to tear them up. See, she took everything with her: all her clothes, her books, pictures, everything. Her shoes. Those notes were all she left behind. I couldn't bring myself to get rid of them, at first. But they were driving me out of my mind. And what if someone came over, a client or something, and saw them all over the house. It was crazy. Those goddamn notes almost drove me crazy.

from

Chronic
by Linda Griffiths

Premiered at the Factory Theatre, Toronto, produced by Duchess
Productions, 2003, directed by Simon Heath. Script available from
Playwrights Canada Press.

• • •

*Petra, a web designer in her thirties, comes down with
a mysterious illness which infects both people and computers.
It's a virus, played by a VIRUS. He is the smoothest, funniest,
smartest, nastiest, sexiest, scariest character in the play. He is
Petra, a replicant version—a demon lover, he's around every
corner of her psyche, waiting to reproduce.*

VIRUS

The body forgets nothing. Not a single negative thought, not when you
dreamt your own funeral as a child, not any carnage you've ever seen. It's
martoonie time, it's martoonie time. The father started saying things at
about the second martini. He'd go at the mother and at her and at her,
humiliating her. "You're slurring your words. You can't handle two drinks,
just have one." For some reason, the mother couldn't say, "piss off." She
could only imagine passive resistance. So, with money she's saved from
her housekeeping allowance, she bought her own bottle of gin, her own
vermouth, her own jar of olives and she hid the bottles in the pockets of
her old fur coat in the hall cupboard. Just before the father came home, she
would mix herself one cocktail, drink it all alone, then wash the glass and
put it away. When the father came home, he'd have two martinis and she
would have one. Only the daughter knew. Don't tell your father. Each bad
thought lets the intruder in. You're incomparably smug, having a good day,
then you think of doing taxes and that throttle of fear comes, your immune
system fails. You try not to think that thought and the trying is lying, and
that leads to more negative thinking, the thoughts gather momentum, your
affirmations, your visualizations, your teen images, are like a pinky finger
in a contaminated dike, holding back a sea of little blind beasts with open
mouths, yakking to each other, telling the cell to produce thousands,

millions of new intruders, they're sucking, tearing away bits of the cell's protective membrane, exulting in their own reproduction. Love me. Accept me. That's all I want. To be your co-traveller through life.

from

Beat the Sunset
by Michael Lewis MacLennan

Premiered at the Kaleidoscope Playhouse, Victoria, produced by Company Epidêmos, 1993, directed by Michael Lewis MacLennan. Script available from Playwrights Canada Press.

• • •

> *SACHA is a professor specializing in the history of epidemics. He addresses his class, having recently found out that his high school friend Adam has returned to the city, sick with AIDS.*

SACHA

Before we close our first class, I want you to imagine that there is an epidemic in which a disease rapidly weakens the body and shuts down the immune system. This enables other diseases to invade the body. You lie there feverish, soaked in sweat and dying of some combination of diseases specific only to you, preying on your weakened body and soon, killing you.

And this disease seems to have… preferences… about who it infects and kills.

And imagine that the people who die most are pregnant women and children. Pregnant women lose any immunity to the disease. And it takes children five years to develop the antibodies to have a fighting chance against the disease.

And imagine that when it hits men, the fevers reach 104 degrees, temperatures at which sperm cooks. So if you survive, you're probably infertile.

So you have this disease where it's harder and harder for men and women to conceive children in the first place. Then, if the disease doesn't knock off the wife and her fetus, it's likely to press the little one into the ground before he or she is five years old. Makes it hard to have a family. Makes you think—wow, that's some intelligent disease, it sure knows what it's doing.

And if you followed human nature,
if you were a God-fearing type,

you just might think, hey,
this is God's wrath we're seeing,
and it's wrath against heterosexuals.
It's wrath against traditional family values.
It's a sure sign.

The thing is, this disease exists. It has wreaked havoc for all recorded time, on every continent. This isn't a fable. Know what it is? Malaria.

Malaria has killed half of the men and women and children that have ever died on this planet. Fifty percent of all deaths, ever, have been caused by malaria. And now, every year, it takes residence in the bodies of nearly six-hundred million people, burying one million—almost the population of Vancouver—one million African infants each year.

All this from the plasmodium parasite,
the smallest animal on earth.

I wish it were a fable, but it isn't.

from

The Crackwalker
by Judith Thompson

Premiered at Theatre Passe Muraille, Toronto, 1980, directed by Clarke Rogers. Script available from Playwrights Canada Press.

• • •

ALAN asks for help in getting the "snakes" out of his head.

ALAN

Did you ever start thinkin something, and it's like ugly…? And ya can't beat it out of your head? I wouldn't be scared of it if it was sittin in front of me, I'd beat it to shit—nothing wouldn't stop me—but I can't beat it cause it's in my head fuck. It's not like bein crazy, it's just like thinkin one thing over and over and it kinda makes me sick. Like when I was a kid and I used to have these earaches all the time, you know? And I would keep thinkin it was like a couple of garter snakes with big ugly teeth all yellow, like an old guy's teeth and there they were the two of them suckin and bitin on my eardrum with these yellow teeth. Makin noises like a cat eatin cat food. I could even hear them fuckin noises. *(makes the noise)* Like that. Just made me wanta puke thinkin that—made the pain worse. I'd think of their eyes, too, that made me sick, black eyes lookin sideways all the time while they keep suckin and chewin on my eardrum. Fuck. Do youse know what I mean? No offense or nothin I don't mean no offense I wish youse all good luck in your lives. I was just—like I just wanted to know if any of youse like knew of a medicine or somethin ya might take for this—they gotta have somethin cause the one I'm thinkin of now is even worse it's fuckin bad, it's it's somethin Bonnie Cain told me about this nurse she knows goin out to Enterprise out to one of the farms out there these folks were on the dole so she goes up to see if the kids got colds and that, and the wife, all small with her teeth all black takes her into the warsh room and tells her she got somethin wrong down in her woman's part. And Bonnie said this nurse lifted up this woman's skirt and you know what she seen? Like a cauliflower growin out of her thing! A cauliflower! Fuck! And ya know the worst part of it? When ya cut it it bleeds! It grows blood and that! It just happened last summer too, last fuckin summer in July!… How'd she

go—like how'd she pee? Fuck I'll be doin the dishes where I'm workin
down the Tropicana there and it's like pictures burning holes in my brain
I try all the time to like put other pictures over top of that, nice things that
I really get off on, eh, that I really like like—like lambs in a field, whenever
I see one in a field or someplace I always laughed at them so stupid lookin
and cute fuck—I never told the other guys they were there case they burn
them or something. Anyways I try putting pictures of these baby sheep
over top of the cauliflower and I'll do it and it's okay for a second then the
lamb its eye'll go all funny like slits lookin sideways just like them snakes
and then it'll open its mouth and there'll be them long sharp teeth and
a bunch of worms inside and the nice little sheep goes all ugly on me
and the cauliflower comes back worse than ever like it ate the sheep or
somethin…. Maybe if I could just have a car or get back to workin on cars,
you know? Or get into Dragmasters, then maybe I'd stop thinkin of these
things. I don't know. I'm looking for somebody who knows, that's why I'm
askin youse I don't know. I wish I did. *(pause)* If it was in front of me I'd
beat it to shit, you know?

from

The Collected Works of Billy the Kid:
Left Handed Poems
by Michael Ondaatje

Premiered at Neptune Theatre, Halifax, 1975, directed by John Wood. Available from House of Anansi Press.

• • •

BILLY is alone, talking about a time he laid low to recuperate from a fever.

BILLY

The barn I stayed in for a week then was at the edge of a farm and had been deserted it seemed for several years, though built of stone and good wood. The cold dark grey of the place made my eyes become used to soft light and I burned out my fever there. It was twenty yards long, about ten yards wide. Above me was another similar-sized room but the floors were unsafe for me to walk on. However I heard birds and the odd animal scrape their feet, the rotten wood magnifying the sound so they entered my dreams and nightmares.

But it was the colour and light of the place that made me stay there, not my fever. It became a calm week. It was the colour and the light. The colour a grey with remnants of brown—for instance those rust brown pipes and metal objects that before had held bridles or pails, that slid to machine uses; the thirty or so grey cans in one corner of the room, their ellipses, from where I sat, setting up patterns in the dark.

When I had arrived I opened two windows and a door and the sun poured blocks and angles in, lighting up the floor's skin of feathers and dust and old grain. The windows looked out onto fields and plants grew at the door, me killing them gradually with my urine. Wind came in wet and brought in birds who flew to the other end of the room to get their aim to fly out again. An old tarp hung from the roof, the same colour as the walls, so once I knocked myself out on it.

For that week then I made a bed of the table there and lay out my fever, whatever it was. I began to block my mind of all thought. Just sensed the room and learnt what my body could do, what it could survive, what colours it liked best, what songs I sang best. There were animals who did not move out and accepted me as a larger breed. I ate the old grain with them, drank from a constant puddle about twenty yards away from the barn. I saw no human and heard no human voice, learned to squat the best way when shitting, used leaves for wiping, never ate flesh or touched another animal's flesh, never entered his boundary. We were all aware and allowed each other. The fly who sat on my arm, after his inquiry, just went away, ate his disease and kept it in him. When I walked I avoided the cobwebs who had places to grow to, who had stories to finish. The flies caught in those acrobat nets were the only murder I saw.

And in the barn next to us there was another granary, separated by just a thick wood door. In it a hundred or so rats, thick rats, eating and eating the foot-deep pile of grain abandoned now and fermenting so that at the end of my week, after a heavy rainstorm burst the power in those seeds and brought drunkenness into the minds of those rats, they abandoned the sanity of eating the food before them and turned on each other and grotesque and awkwardly because of their size went for each other's eyes and ribs so the yellow stomach slid out and they came through the door and killed a chipmunk—about ten of them onto that one striped thing and the ten eating each other before they realized the chipmunk was long gone so that I, sitting on the open window with its thick sill where they couldn't reach me, filled my gun and fired again and again into their slow wheel across the room at each boommm, and reloaded and fired again and again till I went through the whole bag of bullet supplies—the noise breaking out the seal of silence in my ears, the smoke sucked out of the window as it emerged from my fist and the long twenty-yard space between me and them empty but for the floating bullet lonely as an emissary across and between the wooden posts that never returned, so the rats continued to wheel and stop in the silences and eat each other, some even the bullet. Till my hand was black and the gun was hot and no other animal of any kind remained in that room but for the boy in the blue shirt sitting there coughing at the dust, rubbing the sweat of his upper lip with his left forearm.

from

The Monument
by Colleen Wagner

Premiered at the Canadian Stage Company, Toronto, co-produced by
Necessary Angel Theatre Co. and the Manitoba Theatre Centre, 1995,
directed by Richard Rose. Script available from Playwrights Canada Press.

• • •

*STETKO and Mejra stand in the forest. The lighting has
gradually changed to indicate the passing of time and a change
of location. They are now deeper in the forest—it's darker, the
shadows are longer. STETKO comes to the mass grave where the
bodies have been buried, and after some pressure from Mejra,
recalls the last day he spent with the "one he liked the most."*

STETKO

I was driving the jeep.
I was laughing.
Finally I was alone.
I got to drive on my own—with her
this girl.
It felt really good.
The sun was shining the whole time.
I was singing
I'm finally alone with this girl.
And I'm singing—

> *He sings a popular song.*

I look over at her
and she's not smiling
just looking straight ahead.
I'd forgot you see,
I forgot what I supposed to be doing—
killing them.

I forgot.
I was suddenly a free man going for a ride with my girl.

Then everything got serious.
I don't remember anything until we get here
and I tell her to lift her arms up over her head.
And she does.
I tie her hands together and throw the rope over the tree branch.
It's gone now.
Somebody has cut it down.

I pull the rope til she's stretched as far as she can go
and
then I pull til she's just off the ground.
She looks so pretty.
Big watery eyes
like a doe's
I cut her dress—
because her hands are tied and I can't get it off otherwise.
I use my hunting knife.
She's got very white skin.
It's never seen the sun.
She's got a thin line of black hairs that run up to her belly button.
I think it's quite sexy.
I tell her so.
I go up to her
and
put my arms around her
and kiss her neck.
I figure I can do it with her.
I feel her shiver.
I ask her if she's cold.
She says "no."
I ask her if she's afraid.
She shakes her head
but I think she's lying.
I ask her if she wants me to undress—
maybe she hasn't seen a man before
naked.
She closes her eyes

tight.
So I tell her I won't take my clothes off
and she opens them again
and I can see she's crying.

So I stop
and sit down on a log
or rock
and I tell her about myself
and my uncle.
I tell her about my girlfriend.

I ask her what she wants to be when she grows up.
She says she wants to be a teacher.
I tell her she's just like my girlfriend
wanting to put some good back into the world.
I tell her I would too
if I knew how.

I tell her she's beautiful.
I tell her I want to do it with her.
I figure maybe I can come with her.

She begs me not to
but I try anyway.

Only I can't.
I can't get hard.
It won't go in.
I can't do it anymore.

It's all over.

                    Pause.

I don't know what to do.

She begs me to set her free.
And I'm thinking "what if I do?"
What if I set her free. What will happen?
I'm scared—in case the others find out—
They'd kill me for letting the enemy go.

She says she won't tell anyone.

I notice her hands are swollen and white.
It's getting late
the sun's going down
I have to return the jeep.

So I leave it to fate.
I say, Let's see if she's meant to live.

I back away
and
close my eyes
and aim the gun
and I say to myself
if I miss
no matter what,
I let her go.

Pause.

It hit her in the face.

Silence.

from

cherry docs
by David Gow

Premiered at Factory Theatre, Toronto, produced by Volcano, 1998, directed by Richard Rose. Script available from Scirocco Drama.

• • •

DANNY's last monologue.

DANNY

I'm driving on Bloor Street. I'm in my Volvo. I'm trying to drive fast. I'm at Bathurst. I stop at a red light. Some kids try to clean my windshield with their little squeegees, buckets of waste water. Their "uniforms" are confusing to me. Twenty-one different colours of hair, in different forms. Metal, pierced through lips, leather. An atrocious array of clothing. What does it mean? Who are these strange people? Punks of some sort. A swastika with a red circle and a line through it. No smoking? *(short pause)* No Nazis? *(pause)* Why is my reaction to their wanting to clean my windshield so visceral and frankly violent? *(pause)* I wanted a small piece of... redemption for Michael so badly, I was willing to beat it out of him with the broken back of Elijah's chair. *(pause)* These seven threads comprise a cloth: Spirit, Light, Time, Space, Birth, Death and the Seventh Thread which is the Mystery of the Universe. The un-nameable name which enlivens the dance. This Seventh Thread is also the opposite of Spirit, the opposite of Light, the opposite of Time, the opposite of Space, the opposite of Birth, the opposite of Death. *(pause)* It is only the interplay, the movement between all these threads, which creates the Dimensional Known and Unknown Universe. The Seven-threaded Dimensional cloth, which is the very fabric of the Un-nameable. The Fabric extending out from any point, of our Universe. *(pause)* The fabric must always be free to move, the threads must interweave and dance through one another; in all their dimensions. That is the only richness in the fabric. *(pause)* This movement, this animation in the cloth is: *The Divine Dance of Eternity.* *(pause)* I'm on Bloor Street, in my car. Water streams down my windshield. Sudsy and grey, tired water of a thousand washings. I go to hit the wiper switch arm, to get these fucking kids off my car. What am I thinking? I hate these kids; no, not exactly, I'm afraid of them. Then, self loathing. I look at them in all their ugliness, in all their confusion, in all their begging state, and I try to reserve judgment on their lives; on my own life; on that of Michael; on those of they I know, and I leave it to another.

from

Three in the Back, Two in the Head
by Jason Sherman

Premiered at the Tarragon Theatre, Toronto, co-produced by Necessary Angel Theatre Company, Tarragon Theatre, and the National Arts Centre, 1994, directed by Richard Rose. Script available from Playwrights Canada Press.

. . .

"The Week in Review"

> *CIA agent John DOYLE burrows into the mind of Paul Jackson, the son of a military scientist who was murdered on DOYLE's orders.*

DOYLE

"Do something," you said, "protect me." And he did. Protected you. Your mother. Your daughter.

I know all about you, Paul. You are separated, one child, a reasonable mortgage; weekdays, a conductor of classes, speaker of lectures; poker every second Friday with your university friends; Saturday nights you get drunk and call your wife and ask if you could come home now; on Sunday, you read *The New York Times*, your favourite section, "The Week in Review." You see pictures there of war and death and you wonder what you can do to stop it, but you realize, in your heart, you don't give a damn really, not enough to want to do something to stop it, not really enough at all, because now you don't give a damn about the peasants and the poor, the refugees and the victims of torture, you have your life, it has been given to you and you like it, you are in love with your life and you want nothing to disturb the stillness of it, and if you are to have your life, the lectures and the poker and the sentimental drunkenness of it, you realize that there must be the poor and the peasants and the victims of torture, *fuck them.* You have your child and you love her very much, and the only reason your heart aches for the dying and dead children of war is that you see in their faces the face of your own daughter, you want to protect her, your own, not the others, and that is what your father taught us, protect your own, your *own*, not *them*; at this watering hole, fight to protect your own.

You'll give me the bag. I'll take the contents of the bag. There will be an inquiry into the activities of your father. It will be made clear that he was victimized, that, twenty-five years ago, his work on space defense was sabotaged, and that the saboteur was Ed Sparrow. Ed Sparrow faked tests. Ed Sparrow lied to Congress, and to this nation, his own people. It is Ed Sparrow who will be humiliated. It is Ed Sparrow who will be seen to have betrayed this nation. And, as his name sinks, your father's name will rise, *rise*, and, once we have built Snowman, it will soar into space. Paul… you will give me the bag.

from

Tightrope Time: Ain't Nuthin' More Than Some Itty Bitty Madness Between Twilight & Dawn
by Walter Borden

Premiered at the Centaur Theatre, Montreal, 1987, directed by Frederick Edell. Script available from Playwrights Canada Press.

• • •

"Git it out your system"

In one of the many chambers in the mansions of the "Host's" mind, the MINISTER OF DEFENSE is found spewing his radical activism designed to alleviate the Black man's burden.

MINISTER OF DEFENSE

I recall how just the other day this white man had the nerve to say to me: sir, he says, life is a banquet; enjoy yourself. Well, I looks this fool right into his eye and I says: sir, how many times have we been led to the banquet table only to be told we could get our victuals in the kitchen?

How many times have we watched you wrap your lips around the giblets of sweet contentment while we have been asked to gnaw upon the drumstick of despair? How many times, I said, are we to be forced to accept the chocolate and not the mousse?

Well that same idiot looked at me with this Simple Simon grin across his face and said: My goodness, sir, I could be wrong, but you seem somewhat perplexed. What possibly could be the matter?

You can take your matters and you can shove your matters right on up your ass, I said. We will no longer be deceived. It is the eleventh hour—and the heat is on! We are ready to do whatever is necessary to redeem our right to sit down at the banquet of life with the rest of the human family. We are prepared to fight, and fight we will!

We will fight you on the street corners,
And in the pool halls.
We will fight you on the dance floors,
And at the back of the bus.

We will fight you on the football fields,
And at Bingo—
We will fight—
We will fight you at the welfare office,
And in the taverns,
We will fight you at the poker tables
And on the basketball courts.

WE WILL NEVER SURRENDER!

from

Wacousta
by James Reaney

Premiered at the General Amherst High School, Amherstburg, Ontario, produced by NDWT. Co., 1978, directed by Keith Turnbull. Script available from Playwrights Guild of Canada.

• • •

> *A dramatic retelling of the giant Wacousta's revenge on the British garrison at Detroit and Michilimackinac taken from the 1832 writing of Major John Richardson.*

PONTIAC

I, Pontiac, was an opponent to the English… these dogs dressed in red who came with their forts and their guns and their whiskey to rob us of our hunting grounds and drive away the game.

A message I received in a vision granted me from the Master of Life. "Lift the hatchet against the English and wipe them from the face of the earth." Serpents, harpies… the English red coat hunting dogs have set eggs in our hunting grounds, eggs which they call forts… nine serpent eggs. Fort Niagara, Sandusky, Venango, Presquile, Miami, St. Joseph, Schlosser, Michilimackinac… Détroit. These nine eggs are filled with straight lines, free-ways, heartlessness, long knives, minuets, harpsichords, hoopskirts, death, disease, right-angled extermination.

One by one, under my leadership, we crushed their forts before they could sit on them long enough to hatch their murderous culture. Niagara, Sandusky, Venango, Presquile, Miami, St. Joseph, Schlosser…

All save these two… Michilimackinac… *(pausing)* Détroit.

In forts, tough, hard-faced foreign devils, worshippers of the sky-demon Jehovah, shut their gates fast—hermetically sealed.

After twelve months they have divided my Ottawas from my allies the Potawatomies and the Delawares. With offers of a separate peace. Shall we think of peace too for a while? Shall we also smoke the white calumet with these foreign devils or shall we make one last lunge against these two remaining serpent eggs—Michilimackinac... *(pausing)* Détroit. Who will speak for peace?

from

The League of Nathans
by Jason Sherman

Premiered at Theatre Passe Muraille, Toronto, produced by Orange Dog Theatre, 1992, directed by Ian Prinsloo. Script available from Playwrights Canada Press.

• • •

"He's Talking About That Thing"

Nathan of Winnipeg can't understand why his beloved Israel would bomb the shit out of Lebanon.

ISAACS

He's talking about... that thing... how it's an act of desperation—kids, with no future, kids, living in these refugee camps, no jobs, no sewage, no nothin'. Then—he says he's leaving the synagogue, he's quitting being a Rabbi. He says he's been thinking about it a long time, and he's come to the realization that Israel "being the way it is," he cannot "in all good conscience continue to be a Rabbi." Said you can't have both, Judaism and Zionism in the same place. Said they're "diametrically opposed." Then, he takes off his tallis, lays it over the Torah. People gasped, like *(gasps)* like that. Then he walked out, right up the centre aisle. Total fuckin' silence. I called him up the next day, went over to see him in his little apartment. He was packin'. Getting ready to move to Israel. "After what you just did in the *shul*, you're going to Israel?" He goes, "I'm going to make sure the Jews stay Jewish." Then he dug out this scrapbook, all kinds of pictures he'd been keeping about Israel, like a whole history I'd never seen before. Had this one section on Lebanon. Beirut blown to shit, refugee camps. And this one picture, of a little girl, couldn'ta been more than four. A fuckin' angel, with these huge eyes, just this perfect little girl. Then I see her leg is in a cast. A bomb tore her foot off. A bomb knocked her house down. A bomb killed her family. An Israeli bomb. A Jewish bomb. He says to me, "Who do you think did this?" Before I can say anything, he goes, "We did." You and me and him and all of us. "The money we send to Israel," he says, "killed this little girl's family. And our silence maimed her." Fuckin' floored me. I mean, the guy's saying that the money I send, the cheque I write, the, the bonds

I buy, is what allowed this to happen. I go, "Well, I don't know what to do. All these years I'm thinking I'm doing the right thing and you're telling me—I mean, what do I do? I go to Israel with you, what?" He says, "No. You don't have to go to Israel. You can fight them right here. Just raise your voice. Ask questions."

from

Wedding Day at the Cro-Magnons'
by Wajdi Mouawad
translated by Shelley Tepperman

Premiered at the National Arts Centre Atelier, Ottawa, 1996, directed by
Bañuta Rubess. Script available from Playwrights Canada Press (English)
and Leméac Éditeur (French).

• • •

"The Soldier-Poet"

> WALTER, *a young soldier, renowned for his killing prowess,
> arrives at his sister's wartime wedding, his enemies in pursuit.
> Exhausted, he throws his gun out the window.*

WALTER

Soldiers, catch my machine gun, shoot me with it if you like! (*He starts
to take off his cartridge belt and pouches, and bit by bit, his whole warrior's
outfit.*) You've always dreaded me, you've dreaded my fury and my strength,
my thirst for your blood. My name became flashing neon in your brains,
and after squabbling amongst yourselves for the honour of killing me,
you're still the ones dropping at my feet. But where's the beauty I was born
for? Horror isn't an inviting realm and yet, for years I've killed those who
didn't see me in time and I was the eagle who left food for the vultures and
crows! I am Walter! I remember your rage and your pain, I remember your
promises and your threats! For you my name was a country to conquer,
a tree to fell! Walter! The sun shone less in your eyes than the first letter of
my name! So go ahead, kill me, kill me... I'm the murderer of your dreams,
I'm the killer, the swallower of herds, the snatcher of fish. Kill me! Go on!
Shoot! But aim well; I'm not fighting anymore, I'm not fighting, I'm not
fighting anymore.

In the darkness, the birds
retreat into the chimney
fire in the blue
A storm is resting
On the back of the mountain

The lilies are still
In the tomblike silence
a reassuring presence
for the night hunter on foot.
In the distance, a face takes flight.
Further along, the sea is calm;
Long ago, the sun would find its way there
The way is white
And trimmed with gold.
And the lambs are still asleep in the fields.
Violet glides across the plains
To pick the morning roses.
In the autumn they fall
The leaves fall
And the rain falls with them.
Today I walk,
I walk, and in my head
And in my heart
I remember!
A love is born.
At the detour of a road
I kissed her lips.
The day has risen.
Four willows intertwine in the blue
In my hands, your marvelous face!
How can I tell you of my terror
Without tearing myself apart?
A thousand times better to tear myself apart
Than to keep it inside me and bury it!
The white sash of day slides across the pond
Overtakes the villages,
and stretches beyond,
Three birds take flight!
I smile,
I smile,
I smile with joy.

from

Two Words for Snow
by Richard Sanger

Premiered at the Alberta Theatre Projects' playRites Festival, Calgary, 1999.
Script available from Red Deer Press.

• • •

The Explorers' Club, New York, 1910. The polar explorer Robert Edwin PEARY, 53, is pushed out in a wheelchair by his seven-year-old son. In the eighteen months since his allegedly successful expedition to the North Pole, he has aged greatly. He is now preparing to appear before congressional hearings to determine whether he or his rival Dr. Frederick Cook reached the Pole. This is not how he imagined his return to civilization. PEARY will take Captain Bob Bartlett of Newfoundland with him to the hearings, betraying the promise he made to his African-American assistant, Matthew Henson, to recognize his faith and loyalty.

PEARY

I'll tell them the truth.

The one rule I know: Take. A gentleman's word is his bond—No. Find a way or make one—No. Take. Take. Take the North Pole. They don't know what it takes but I do. It takes a special man, it took modern science and Eskimo know-how, it took meteorites and money, yes, generously donated, it took lives, even American lives, to reach, to conquer, yes, to take the North Pole. I know because it took me, I took it, I took the prize (*pulls a caramel out of his pocket*). Yes, only eighteen months ago, I did, and now they are taking it from me, Bobby. Yes, they are, in their meanness and envy. Don't let them do that to you.

Hah! What do you have that they would take from you? Shot a squirrel, did you? Have you stuffed it? No! If you don't stuff it, they'll take it from you and they will keep taking for the rest of your life…. That's why we have taxidermy, that's why we have photographs. Get your jack-knife out and skin it.

They will take it from you, just like they took my prize from me. I took them there, I took America there, I took my coloured bodyservant, I took the Eskimo, and they were happy. Happy to take the salaries I paid them, to take the gifts I gave them, the knives, the biscuits, the rifles, the means of navigation.... And that was all well and fine, I didn't mind. But then it was not right what they began to take: my rations, my route, my caramels, my prize—

It was my expedition, I raised the money. Six figures, a one with five zeros, one hundred thousand dollars—Bartlett? Are you listening? I was the first, the upright single digit, and they five shadows following, which when we returned, oh when we turned to come back, turned to crows, to vultures and took flight. They turned on me, they tried to leave me behind—

No, no, they tried to kill me. And then Dr. Cook joined them and the New York *Herald* and others, and they began to take more, take faster.... They're on to my blood now—

from

The Kabbalistic Psychoanalysis of Adam R. Tzaddik
by Anton Piatigorsky

Premiered at Summerworks, Toronto, 1998, directed by Chris Abraham.
Script available from Playwrights Canada Press.

• • •

*ADAM is an aspiring Jewish mystic and patient in
psycho-analysis. Through therapy, he has begun to question
his religious view of the world, and of himself. He is speaking
to his psychiatrist.*

ADAM

A number of years ago, I went to Israel with my family. I was sitting in the
streets of Safed alone, while my parents and sister went to sightsee Isaac
Luria's synagogue. An old black-hatted Hasid sat down next to me and
asked me my name. I told him Adam R. Tzaddik. His face lit up and he
looked at me like I was somebody. My son, he scolded, with a name like
that you've got to move to Israel! The initials, see. In Hebrew. Adam begins
with Aleph. R in Hebrew is the letter Resh. And Tzaddik begins with the
letter Tzaddie. Aleph, Resh, Tzaddie. Spells Eretz. In Hebrew, eretz means
land. The land of Israel, Eretz, the one true land.

ADAM laughs.

You, of all people, my son, your presence belongs in Eretz Yisrael! He's
all bloated and excited. These guys… I tell you… *(pause)* I said… I said,
I don't speak Hebrew. Aleph, Resh, Tzaddie. Whatever. The name's Adam
with and "A" and Tzaddik with a "T". And if you wanna play name games
I'm A-R-T art, that's what. *(pause)* I really liked that guy. I mean, he was
something else. The way he looked at me. Like I held the whole future in
my hands because of my name. Giving a shit about me for no other reason
than my name. These religious people and their words, their deep care for
the words… *(pause)* Adam R. Tzaddik. I'm here, in this body, this name,
and I don't speak Hebrew, not very well, and though I've tried so hard to
reach for God all I've studied is myself. This conflict container and jumble
of Freudian clichés. Pre-civilized thoughts, desire for the kin. That's the

story of my life. Not the Zohar. That. It's such small drama, so barely kitchen sink. Behold the man, pre-scripted, pre-fabricated! Easy-to-assemble mythology man, comes parts complete. All packed into this miserable thing. This language, this name, this... English, room, couch. Here in these things, somewhere Adam, here. In this thing.

My God, what is this? This body, this mythological shell? This breathing, eating, digesting, farting, fucking, bleeding mass of blob? This horrible object? This "I"? what the hell am I?

from

Provenance
by Ronnie Burkett

Premiered at the Theatre Network, Edmonton, 2003. Script available from
Playwrights Canada Press.

• • •

*TENDER, a young Canadian soldier serving overseas in World
War I, relives his death.*

TENDER

When I awoke I saw the dawn, the ringing in my ears was gone, and
morning's mist was all around. There was no sound, but this. The crunch
of fallen leaves under footsteps coming near. Not an army like before, nor
the sound of distant war, just one man walking toward me as I lay there on
the forest's floor. "Are you hurt?" he asked, and I said no, simply taking rest.
"I will not be addressed that way, stand up, salute, explain yourself, what
have you to say?" I stumbled to my feet to find a man whose age and rank
were greater than my own. Not a boy, nor a soldier toy, he was an officer
from the army of men, different, better, higher, yes, but also from my home.
He was me, he was mine, familiar and living and true, but when I reached
out for his hand he struck me down again. "Look at you!" he spit, his foot
was on my chest. "A coward running through the woods, a runaway, no less.
You will not defile those clothes anymore, will not ridicule these garments
of war. Stand up, strip down, undress!" I tried to speak again, to tell the hell
I saw, but when I moved my mouth his fist was swift and hit my jaw. I bled
at last in war, beaten by my own. "Coward, coward, coward" he crowed, as
my uniform hit the ground. Blood and leaves and tartan swirled all around.
I was not his brother, his comrade or his friend.

A naked boy in foreign wood, cloaked in shame and autumn air. Not
a man, nor a toy, neither soldier, just a boy. Shivering, hairless, pale and
lost, waiting for this jury of one to speak the price, extract the cost for
running from death to this. From his rucksack the man took something
soft, something green, and threw it in my face. It smelled of something
beautiful, the city, a woman, powder, life lived far from this strange place.
"If you can't be a man" he said, "then you must be a girl. Hairless and pale

and afraid. But you're less than a girl, so put on these stockings and then you'll be made like the whores I took them from in Paris." And for a moment, he smiled and was delicate as I fumbled with the silk, embarrassed by his game. I was not a toy soldier, but a doll yet again. He knelt between my legs and smoothed the green shroud as it enveloped my skin, touching only stocking, never flesh, no part of me on him. And slowly standing, turned me round and bent me toward a tree. The bark was rough against my cheek, but not so coarse as his trouser's wool, scratching at my back, rubbing against me.

And then, I bled again. Ripped wide by what, I did not know. Oh no, oh no, not that, not him in me. His hands on my hips, pounding from the rear. I screamed, but no one heard, only trees were near. "Coward, coward, worse than a girl" he whispered as he took me at the tree. This was not love, this was not sweet, a little toy soldier's final defeat. This was not beautiful, I am not your Christ. No God cried for me as this son paid the price. No poppy grows to resurrect me, as my countryman fucked me and finished my youth. Who was the coward now, there is your truth. Brave soldier he was, and honoured back home, butchered a boy, buggered his own. Sing him a song, he knows all the words. And a secret verse you never have heard. "Coward, coward, worse than a girl," everyone sing along.

The melody of me will not linger on. You will not remember my name.

Arms overhead, left for dead, forgotten little soldier boy, tied up to the tree. Cast-off broken soldier's whore, toyed with in the leaves. A carpet of red and gold underneath my feet, branches blazing with their dead ready for release. But I cannot return to dirt and rot into the ground, for I am held against the bark, no earthly grave to mark the spot where the little toy soldier fell down.

from

Not Spain
by Richard Sanger

Premiered at Theatre Passe Muraille, Toronto, 1996, directed by Naomi Campbell and Deborah Lambie. Script available from Playwrights Canada Press.

. . .

"Carousel"

> *War has torn apart the city where ANDREI lives. While he is helping a neighbour move a freezer full of food across the city, a shell explodes very nearby. ANDREI falls to the ground.*

ANDREI

I see the road very close up for a long time. It's chalky pale-yellow limestone, with bits of broken cinder blocks and rock and a shiny belt-buckle right near my nose and some broken black plastic. Then there's a noise—my neck hurts but I look from the corner of my eye and then hide my face in the road. It's four soldiers coming up the hill behind me, with big boots that crunch, they are coming closer, they are singing "*Deux milles à pied, ça use, ça use—*" and just when the chorus ends, one kicks me in the ribs. "*Ça use les SOULIERS!*" UGH. And they march on.

Behind them comes an older man, with a crutch, and he cries "Wait for me! Wait for me! I'm the dead Goran's father! Wait!" But one of the boys just throws a stone at him and says, "Get lost, Grandad." And behind him I hear a woman crying "You promised, you promised," but he doesn't answer, and she goes by dragging two big suitcases. And there are lots of people, they are speaking and screaming and sobbing, and some are dragging metal on the stones, but I don't see them, I keep very still. And then it's quiet, and far-off I hear a woman's voice singing an old song from the mountains:

> *Sings:*

Three brothers are building a city;
King John, Count Mark, and George.

They are building the city of Talar,
There where the river roars.

I look and there's an old woman in a shawl pushing a wheelbarrow slowly
up the hill, like she's in no rush, like this, going from side to side. She is
singing and at the same time talking in a low voice to something in the
wheelbarrow, a baby or maybe an animal. But about ten yards beyond me,
she stops. Something has fallen from the wheelbarrow. She picks it up—
I see it's an arm with lots of hair and blood and bone—she looks it over
closely, and drops it back onto the road, and then she continues on up the
hill, humming that song.

   Sings:

They build the tower, they build the square,
The streets, the gates, the wall.
They build the city stone by stone,
And soon they've built it all.

from

cherry docs
by David Gow

Premiered at Factory Theatre, Toronto, produced by Volcano, 1998, directed by Richard Rose. Script available from Scirocco Drama.

• • •

Several months after MIKE has been placed in solitary confinement.

MIKE

Hey-hey-hey- hey- hey-ho- ho- ho- ho- ho-oi- oi- oi- oi- oi. Placing the soles of my feet 'gainst one wall, the heals of my hands against the other, nine-by-six, nine-by-six, nine-by-six, nine-by-six... the heels of my hands, the soles of my feet—both walls, facing the floor and *shewt* up-the-wall. Exercise? Ya' could sell it. Up and down. Climb. Up to the top, wet toilet paper on the back-my neck. Soggy wet, toilet paper there. Take it up. Plaster some 'gainst the speaker grill, little too noisy-with-all-the-little-such-and-such. Crawl back down. Keep-it-real-clean-in-here-you-get-away-with-more. Flush the toilet, flush it, flush it over and over. Stainless steel toilet and sink, one piece-it's-a-one-piece-bath-one. Flush it eighteen times, water's cold as ice. Blister cold. Take my shorts, my boxers. Put 'em in there. Cool, cool water-back-the-neck-drive-away-a-headache. Medicine, what's medicine? When ya' got none, nothing. Cold shorts-back-of the neck. Done. Climb back up the wall, fresh wet cold shorts, stuff a corner-shorts in the corner ventilation vent. Humidifier. Humidify the air some. Gotta have games, gotta have somethin'—nuthin else. *(pause)* Now the air's wet, 't's the next day. Now with your thumbnail you can peel moist paint off the old door frame, peel it, scratch it off. Make a little picture, make a little initials. Little scratchy animal. Shave. Face, Head. Half an-hour-forty-five-minute-job. Now it's study time. Look at what Danny said, look at the case, my briefcase. Make a call, collect call to Danny. Fuckin' North Pole freeze-out action here. Fuckin' North Pole. *(pause)* You know what happens when people talk to you like you're stupid. You start acting *really* stupid. You get pretty angry from it. Who knows where it starts? I gotta start somehow.

They never wanted me in with the regular prison population. Too much danger for everyone with me being a "racist" and everything. Nice huh?

from

11places@once
by Sheldon Rosen

Premiered at the Festival of New Work at Playwrights Theatre
Centre, Vancouver, 2006. Script available from the playwright at
srosen1@sympatico.ca.

• • •

> 11places@once *is a large, theatrical meditation-rant about
> being at a crossroads. Eleven simultaneously unfolding stories
> each uniquely bouncing off the trampoline of day-to-day
> existence. In this monologue the central character in this journey
> has become progressively more German over the length of the
> play and here becomes a man named MICHAEL.*

MICHAEL

(slight German accent) Everyone has accumulated secrets over his lifetime.
But I collect other people's secrets as well…. My most intense memory.
Because it was my first secret. The kiss. I saw my mother's kiss. I didn't
know him other than somehow I understood he was a friend of our "Jewish
neighbours" and why they were "Jewish neighbours" rather than just
neighbours. I wasn't sure other than it was the thirties in Berlin and my
parents had to help them in ways small and not so small. And I was very
preoccupied by the white stars they wore outside their homes. I asked my
mother if I could have one but she said only Jewish people could wear
them. I remember being reprimanded in school for drawing a white star
and pinning it to my shirt. But not my sleeve like the others, even though
I had heard someone say once: "He wore his heart on his sleeve," but
I wanted my star on my heart. I glued it to my chest, ruining my best shirt
and nearly destroying my only heart…. A white star on a white shirt. I was
an invisible Jew. A witness to history. What is it that inspires our youthful
fascinations? And then one day, I understood. Six boys ringing a real
Jew. Older than me, but small for his age. *"Juden, juden schwein, juden
schwein."* And they spit on him each time. Where did they get all that spit?
I was not afraid, watching this with my false yellow star on my heart. I was
angry. I was imagining casting out flaming thunderbolts and incinerating

the chanters, their spittle sizzling on their disgusting nine-year-old lips, the way, as I would learn later that poison victims, mouths would burn from the poison. The Jew ran away crying, leaving me to wonder what if it had been me. I prayed to God that I would not be afraid, that I would be fierce in my anger and I would punish them as I had imagined, not run away to the sound of their laughter. Already I was nurturing the seeds that would create the superheroes I would create in my first comic books. I knew already, at the age of six, the kind of man I wanted to be. I took off my star and packed it away for when I was ready…. How easily I digress. So many ghosts behind that door. As I was later reminded in New York, by Miriam Thalberg, the niece of one of the Jewish families just across the street from us on Münchener Strasse. Jews at that time, even before the infamous Kristallnacht, were not allowed to go to the films. In exchange for books, my mother and father would attend the cinema and then immediately come to their flat and perform it for them while it was still dancing in their brains. Often they, or perhaps it was just my mother, would embellish it in ways that made it somewhat grander than perhaps even the film's director had imagined. My parents would normally leave me with Miriam's aunt and uncle. But in the one memory of that time her reminder had awakened, they had taken me as well. Then we all went back to the crowded living room, where my father and mother reenacted the entire film for the extended Thalberg family all gathered in the tiny room. That night it was "La Habanera" with the exquisite Zara Leander, a part my mother was exquisitely suitable for. I played the part of her young mixed-blood son. Apparently, I was impressively earnest in my portrayal. Often the flow was interrupted by my parents' "debates" over what had actually happened. The Thalbergs were as enthralled by these debates as any of the film's primary action. Not that they weren't totally lost in these re-enactments. They certainly had no shortage of need for escaping their reality…. The man my mother kissed was someone connected to these "Jewish neighbours." Perhaps even someone who my father had helped leave the country. I knew it was not the sort of kiss allowed anyone but one's husband. I also knew, that despite the weight of this secret, I could never tell my father, because everything in our life would change if I did. But, I did tell my mother. When she was scolding me for having hit the neighbour's son, Marin. I was clearly not the pacifist that my father was. In my humiliation, I threw the kiss at her like a stone. She went very silent. The very silence that only the end of the world could bring. Tears poised at the entrance to her eyes. She blinked them away—"It is better to erase a wrong with a right than with another wrong, Michael. It is better to forgive than to accuse." I have never revealed a secret since. Nor forgotten one. And later, after her killing, I wondered whether she had kissed the same way the man who had hurt her. This man with his young boy's face that my father took me to meet several years later in the Lower East Side of New York.

from

A Day in the Life of Mordechai Vanunu
by Camyar Chai

Premiered at Performance Works, Vancouver, co-produced by Neworld Theatre and Rumble Productions, 2000, directed by Norman Armour and Andreas Kahre. Script available from Playwrights Canada Press.

• • •

> *Based on true events, MORDECHAI Vanunu is in his thirteenth year of solitary confinement for blowing the whistle on Israel's nuclear arms program. He is in a small cell and is under constant camera surveillance.*

MORDECHAI

(slowly pacing the length of the cell) I dreamt of food last night. In the market. Chewing: fresh bread, coated in the coolness of yogurt, wetting my tongue, dripping down my chin. And then I freshen my mouth with a sprig of parsley like I'm chewing the outdoors. I smell what I eat and it smells of freedom. And then, all of a sudden, I'm riding through a forest smelling freshly rained earth bouncing on the back of a horse holding on to the dancing Arab from the market—the one with the golden tooth. The breeze cooling my face, the crisp air coating my throat and flying through space, swerving around the trees knowing I wouldn't hit any walls. I feel like when I was a little boy. And then the Arab with the golden tooth and I are back in that market in Morocco but it's not Morocco it's Jerusalem. And Cindy is sitting there. Waiting for me. Her smile could light up a pitch-black desert. It makes her little nose crinkle and you see all her freckles. And breasts like pomegranates. Golden Tooth takes me on the back of his horse and every time she is there waiting. I knew him from when I was walking to school. He was a Moslem. At first, I was terrified. Father always said they bite like rabid dogs. I remember his gold tooth. He jumps in the air and dances. When Golden Tooth spins, he flies. Good thing I can't; I'd crush my head on your ceiling here. That's a good trick you've played on me. Imagine that: I'd crush my head from flying, not falling. Imagine that.

You know, I'd really like to put my arm around someone's shoulder. Give someone a bit of encouragement, pat them on the back, kiss them on the forehead. That would be good.

An orange would be nice. Cindy always greeted me with a bag of oranges. She said they reminded her of Florida. "There's a lot more to Florida than Mickey Mouse and Cubans." She has a very sexy voice. Do you think she would find me attractive now? With my rotting teeth and scabby skin? You're a ditzy blond. You're a fucking sentimental Zionist. You know that? You know it's possible to be a Jew and not be a fascist? "Oh yeah, you're one to talk, Mordechai—or is it Motti—the little self-hating Jew."

I loved the smell of her hair. She was a good girl. My mother would love her. "Not yet Motti. I'm too tense here." But, I love your smell. *(He sniffs himself, then speaks to the camera.)* What are you fucking laughing at? You don't think she'd put up with me now? My stink. I smell so bad I can't even get used to it myself. I can see her now. Her soft pink cheeks go stone cold and her eyes shut me out. The same way you look at me now.

I know I should have. Should have done it. Should have done my job. Looked up. Straight up. I would've been a head technician by now. Up the ladder. I could be vacationing in the Mediterranean this time of year.

I lost you. That night in Rome. You told me it's much safer there. You hail a taxi. You seem agitated, in a rush. The cab is speeding towards Rome on the autostrada. I begin to feel uneasy. The atmosphere is tense. I can't breathe. I want to jump out of the car, disappear. I'm scared. Then, I think it's just my imagination. I'm being paranoid. We draw up to an apartment block and we go inside.

My face hits the thick arm of an old couch. I taste the blood from my nose. I feel my arms twisting into a knot. A man's knee pushes into my kidney. I can't breathe. Another man's knee pushes into my groin. I don't want to die. I look up to find you. Cindy, run!

And then you look different.

"I wish my orders were to kill you, you self hating pig. You fucking traitor!"

Then you stab me with a needle.

from

Zastrozzi: The Master of Discipline
by George F. Walker

Premiered at Toronto Free Theatre, Toronto, 1977, directed by William Lane. Script available from Talonbooks.

• • •

ZASTROZZI

I am Zastrozzi. The master criminal of all Europe. This is not a boast. It is information. I am to be feared for countless reasons. The obvious ones of strength and skill with any weapon. The less obvious ones because of the quality of my mind. It is superb. It works in unique ways. And it is always working because I do not sleep. I do not sleep because if I do I have nightmares and when you have a mind like mine you have nightmares that could petrify the devil. Sometimes because my mind is so powerful I even have nightmares when I am awake and because my mind is so powerful I am able to split my consciousness in two and observe myself having my nightmare. This is not a trick. It is a phenomenon. I am having one now. I have this one often. In it, I am what I am. The force of darkness. The clear, sane voice of negative spirituality. Making everyone answerable to the only constant truth I understand. Mankind is weak. The world is ugly. The only way to save them from each other is to destroy them both. In this nightmare I am accomplishing this with great efficiency. I am destroying cities. I am destroying countries. I am disturbing social patterns and upsetting established cultures. I am causing people such unspeakable misery that many of them are actually saving me the trouble of doing away with themselves. And, even better, I am actually making them understand that this is, in fact, the way things should proceed. I am at the height of my power. I am lucid, calm, organized and energetic. Then it happens. A group of people come out of the darkness with sickly smiles on their faces. They walk up to me and tell me they have discovered my weakness, a flaw in my power, and that I am finished as a force to be reckoned with. Then one of them reaches out and tickles me affectionately under my chin. I am furious. I pick him up and crack his spine on my knee then throw him to the ground. He dies immediately. And after he dies he turns his head to me and says, "Misery loves chaos. And chaos loves company." I look at him and even though I know that the dead cannot speak, let alone make sense, I feel my brain turn to burning ashes and all my control run out of my body like mud and I scream at him like a maniac, *(whispering)* "What does that mean."

from

Belle
by Florence Gibson

Premiered at the Factory Theatre, Toronto, 2000, directed by Ken Gass.
Script available from Playwrights Canada Press.

• • •

Belle *is set in the Reconstruction Era of the United States, 1865.*
Belle and BOWLYN, freed slaves, have travelled north to New
York from rural Georgia in search of a new life, only to find even
greater hardships when confronted with the cold, poverty and
racism. Having watched his wife Belle scrub floors, BOWLYN
begins to speak on a street corner in shantytown.

BOWLYN

I will provide for you.
Because I am *MAN*.
It were my *dream* to have a horse and buggy.
(beginning to speak to the passerby)
I had a horse. And that horse was mine. But it was taken from me.
Now I ain't used to speechifyin' my life, but my life is just that: mine. A life
like any other, and so to be honoured. And for that I am tellin' it.
I work always, to raise my family. This is to be the truth of my life—to
provide for my family. Because I am a man.
And because I am a man, I know no man should lead the life I led… back
before freedom… my daddy they'd hire out—*they'd* get paid for his field
work on another farm—*his* work.
But me.
Never could hire me out.
Shut my face like a box lid, white boss screamin', and I would not. Would.
not. *(pause)*
So the bit was placed in my mouth, and the lash put to my back and I was
forced to plough the furrow true as a beast—and yet I was a *man*! *(pause)*
Because I am a man, I have the right to provide for my family, to see my
children fed, my home safe and myself free to serve the country in which
I lie. And I tell you, these are the things that I will do—because I am a man.

from

Salt-Water Moon
by David French

Premiered at the Tarragon Theatre, Toronto, 1984, directed by Bill Glassco. Script available from Talonbooks.

• • •

> *JACOB demands to know from Mary why she would marry the man who humiliated his father.*

JACOB

(bitterly) What cradle will you be using, Mary, once your first child comes? Jerome's old one? That hardwood cradle his father bought him as a child?

> *This stops Mary just as she opens the screen door. She hesitates standing with her back to JACOB.*

It has a lovely antique finish, don't it? Last a lifetime, that cradle. You can set it on the porch on a nice day and rock your first child. Sing him a song to the creak of your foot on the rocker…

> *Mary slams the door, turns and gives JACOB a reproachful, almost defiant, look that makes him turn away.*

…Sing him a sea chanty all about the good ship, *Trinity*, in the summer of '25. How she sailed out of Bay Roberts Harbour in the spring of the year bound for the Labrador and how they struck an east wind and put into Harbour Grace to wait it out. How Captain Abe Wheeler hired a driver to take him back to Bay Roberts, and when he come back two weeks later, the wind was just shifting. All the men, Father included, was in their bunks when the Captain stepped aboard, but he couldn't say a word to the others: they were sharemen. Father was lying there with his boots out over the bedboard, when he heard Captain Abe say, "So this is what you do behind my back, eh, Esau?" "I wasn't doing no harm behind your back," says Father. "We woke up this morning and the day was fair. We done all the work we could." They went up on deck and had more words. Father was not the sort to take dirt from any man. "Go below," says Captain Abe, "and get in the bunk!" "And that I wunt," says Father. "Go below, I said and get in the bunk!" says Captain Abe. "No," says Father, "I wunt." The Captain looked over at Bob Foote. "Bob," he says, "go fetch the constable." Old Bob lowered his eyes and didn't move. "Do as I say, Bob," he says. "Take the punt and fetch the constable." Still Bob wouldn't move.... At last Father said, "No odds, Bob, I'll go below." And he went down and got in his bunk and stayed there till Captain Abe told him to get up. It was either obey or be clapped in jail for six months!...

A lovely sea chanty that every child in Newfoundland should learn by heart? How the *Trinity* came back early that year with a poor catch, and how the merchant looked around for someone to take it out on and his eyes settled on Esau Mercer, the only one who wasn't a shareman, the only one who had crossed the Captain that trip. He marched Father up to his house in Country Road, Will McKenzie did, and brought out the hardwood cradle that belonged to Jerome as a child. He sat Father down in a chair on the porch and told him to rock the cradle, and that's what Father done, day in, day out, from morning till dark, his foot going up and down, up and down on the rocker of that empty cradle, till he was out of collar two months later!...

> *He stands in the yard, his face raised, still trembling from the memory of his father's shame.*

from

The Fisherman's Revenge
by Michael Cook

Premiered with the Newfoundland Travelling Theatre Company, 1976, directed by Dudley Cox. Script available from Playwrights Canada Press.

• • •

Joe, a FISHERMAN, talks about the life he's lived and the things he has seen, but perhaps the happiest memories of all come when he thinks of his daughter, Colleen.

FISHERMAN

I am a poor fisherman, Joe is my name.
All my days I have laboured on the salt water
until my fingers are become knotted as an old fir
and my back bent with hauling.
Time was as a young man, bright and eager,
I would set off on cold mornings
the sun just a thought on the water,
surrounded by my fishing comrades.
Why, the boats were thicker than mackerel
and every one laden with high hearts
looking to a bright future.
Ah me! So many have gone now,
as the fish have gone. Some,
wanting more for their children,
fled to the cities; a few died,
and others simply vanished into air
or so it seemed to me, but then
I am old and foolish and poor
and it is too late now to change—
sooner shift the moon from its cradle
or the stars from their blanket of the dark.
But enough sadness. I am still man enough to joy
aye, and to laugh, and to anger sometimes,

but since my woman died I have been lonely
even though my daughter is a comfort.

      He pauses, take out an old pipe, stuffs it in his mouth.

But soon, she too will be gone, like the swallow,
and that is right, for no girl should do without a man
to turn to in her days and nights.
Her blood is warm, her laughter deep,
and somewhere, amongst stars, unborn children wait for her
I only grieve that I have nothing for her dowry,
save an old clock given me by my mother's mother
some fifty years ago. An old clock!
It has a nice face now, don't mistake me,
but it doesn't go. What use, says I to meself,
what use is a clock that no longer goes?
About as much use as an old fisherman
who has to take his daughter to the nets of a morning
when she should be putting up her hair for the young men...

from

Hosanna
by Michel Tremblay
translated by John Van Burek and Bill Glassco

Premiered at Théâtre de Quat'Sous, Montreal, 1973, directed by André Brassard. Script available from Talonbooks.

• • •

CUIRETTE

For Chrissake, Hosanna, you can smell your fuckin' perfume down the street! All you gotta do is walk by, and you know there's a queer living in the place. You can find the right apartment by just following your nose! Besides, it's a waste of time hiding all your wigs, your gowns, your high-heels, your big sexy David there.... Your old lady never sees 'em anyway. The last time she popped in from Ste-Eustache, remember that, "Surprise, surprise?" I was here then, I saw how you two carried on. We'd just finished supper, eh? I was getting ready to do the dishes, and you were putting on your make-up, remember, 'cause you were going out that night. *In fact*, you were *putting on* your make-up when she walked in the door, Hosanna. You didn't have time to turn your stinkbox here into a "straight" apartment, did you? The whole time she was here, she pretended to see nothing. Not a goddamn thing! After she kissed you she had to take a Kleenex and wipe her mouth 'cause you had pancake all over your face. But she didn't say a word.... And all the time you were farting around in the closet looking for the "basic black number" you were supposed to wear that night, you know where it was? Draped over the only goddamn chair your mother could have sat down in! Still, not a word. Even when I shouted, "Has the mother-in-law arrived?" she didn't hear a thing. Nothing! I did it on purpose too, just to see what she'd do. When you introduced me to her, I had a frying pan in one hand, a dishtowel in the other, and an apron around my waist. And I don't exactly look like a maid, do I, Hosanna! "How do you do," she says in this nice polite voice, but she was looking three feet off to the side.... She only looked at me once.... I got up to take some things out to the kitchen, and when I came back I knew she'd been checking me out 'cause all of a sudden she looked away. And right there, she gave you this sign of approval! Yeah, Hosanna, approval!... As if to say,

"He's very nice, Claude. Your friend is very nice. I approve…." So if it's really true she's coming here tomorrow, and she finds me sleeping in your bed, she's gonna tell you the same thing, Claude, the same thing, "Your friend is very nice. I approve."

from

The Red Priest (Eight Ways to Say Goodbye)
by Mieko Ouchi

Premiered at Alberta Theatre Projects' playRites Festival, Calgary, 2003, directed by Ron Jenkins. Script available from Playwrights Canada Press.

• • •

"A Dream"

This piece was written for and was originally performed with the Largo from "Winter" from "The Four Seasons" by Antonio Vivaldi. VIVALDI, the great Italian violin virtuoso and composer is a year from his death and penniless. He has come to the house of a rich French patron to write a concerto and earn some money. He arrives, only to discover that the patron has made a bet with King Louis XV that VIVALDI cannot teach his young wife to play the violin in six weeks. Through these lessons, VIVALDI has come to know the sad young woman and for the first time, fears for her.

VIVALDI

A dream.

She is dressed in a gown of gold. She is at Versailles. In the Royal Quarters... the suites that no outsider has seen but architects Louis Le Vau and Ange-Jacques Gabriel. I hide myself in the shadows and watch as she steps carefully up the Queen's staircase that leads to the luscious gilt and blossom pink suite of rooms. One wall is covered in tall, ornate glass doors, draped in heavy embroidered silk. She walks towards them and throws one set open.

Ah... the light! The Parterre du Midi.... The Garden. Adorned with statues and fountains. She is staring at something... to the west, at the end of the Royal Walk, sits the Fountain of Apollo. Gold... glorious... bathed in the light of end of day, the sun god rises in his chariot from the water. A chariot so full of life, I can feel the tug of the horses on their bits as it strains to escape into the sky. She begins to run.

I follow her quickly out onto the terrasse… and down the graceful curve of the staircase to the grounds…. She's so far ahead. She has already reached the fountain. A distant figure as she pulls herself onto the thin stone ledge circling the fountain and without a thought. She leaps… towards the water… towards what? Freedom. The water breaks like a slap. I can't seem to see her… I can only imagine her corset tight like a watery embrace pulling her down. I want to save her. I can't seem to move… I'm paralyzed…. Whwa! She breaks through the surface… a swirl of silk and hair and arms…. She fights to move towards the chariot… but… too late. Apollo leaves without her. She screams to him as the chariot lifts off but he, like me, can't seem to hear her cries. I can only watch helplessly like her… his golden cape fluttering behind him as he travels up to the beckoning twilight, disappearing in its darkening embrace.

When I look back down, somehow, she has managed to reach the stone base where the chariot once stood… and pull herself gasping onto it. But as she stands forlornly watching his final ascent… the gold drips off her heavy dress with the water and the dress stiffens where it hangs like ice and she's frozen. She has become a statue. She has replaced him. Amongst the gilded legions of Greek Gods and Goddesses, she alone stands out. A grey, lone statue of a woman.

Made of stone and looking to heaven.

from

Age of Arousal
by Linda Griffiths

Premiering at Alberta Theatre Projects, Calgary, 2007.

• • •

Age of Arousal *is about five Victorian spinsters and one man, EVERARD. The play takes place just as the Suffragette movement is gaining steam. EVERARD dallies with one of the women, a young girl (Monica) he meets in the park. He is rowing Monica on the river Thames as he speaks. The italics indicate he is speaking his thoughts.*

EVERARD

Yes, I believe you are. Just rest, while this great strong man propels you through the waves. *I am striving to be a good man, yet a virile man, to search for my happiness without hurting others, to take pleasure in women because not to do so is to repress one of life's great pleasures, and so I do dally, but often do not taste, I am not at the mercy of my staff, I have practiced the breathing methods of India to control my urges—and yet when I see a woman of a certain shape, a certain smell—all the husbands I know are in a state of abject misery, this bargain is impossible to make and yet I see a woman at my hearth, no not a hearth—in Venice, in Paris—a salon with a woman presiding, giving as good as she gets—could this odd girl become a real woman, a New Woman? I want to embrace my age, the machines and the women, I want to measure and to annotate, perhaps I might even work again if a woman were there to do what they do, to encourage and support, I would let her be free, I am no barbarian to lock a woman up, forbid her to walk alone, yet we would walk together.*

from

Risk Everything
by George F. Walker

Premiered at Theatre Off Park, New York, produced by Rattlestick
Productions, 1997, directed by Daniel De Raey. Script available from
Talonbooks.

• • •

R.J.

Yeah, here it is. Y'know the biggest problem you gotta deal with is the
depressing feeling that hits you when the program is interrupted by
commercials. I mean if you're really into the show it's like life has stopped.
It's that bad. It's that depressing. It's like God has all of a sudden stopped
everything and what are you supposed to do. Just wait? Because that thirty
seconds, that minute, that minute and a half is just like forever. And you
hate those commercials. If you're really into the show you hate them a lot.
And you promise yourself you'll never buy that product. In fact, fuck it,
you don't even pay attention. You don't even wanna know what the product
is. You feel that intense about it… *(He turns the TV off.)* …Yeah. Okay.
(smiles) Anyway it was the sitcom that stopped me from getting really
fucked up about that stuff. When the network started programming
a whole evening of funny shows all together. I mean how strung out can
you get watching light-hearted family entertainment. I even started liking
some of the commercials. Cats in commercials were very big at this time.
Anyway, let's not kid ourselves. This wasn't any golden age of television
comedy. There were no Barney Millers here. No Rhodas. I've seen those
shows on late-night re-runs. And I'm impressed. No, these shows are
mostly about families and everybody talked too loud and only a few of the
jokes ever worked. But it was enough to chill me out. Now those new cop
shows, that's something else. I feel nothing for them. Nothing. Anyway,
everything after "Colombo" is crap. "Colombo," "McCloud," "Hart to Hart,"
"Cagney and Lacey," "Magnum P.I." Shows around that time, they had…
class. I've got a friend who has copies of "Hart to Hart" that he's been
watching for ten years. That's five years in prison and five on the outside
and he's still a loyal fan…. My thing is reality. I first turned into a reality
fan with the afternoon talk shows. But I got hooked…. All those people

with all those problems. It was too much. I got too emotional. Sometimes I couldn't sleep, thinking about those people. So I moved off the talk shows into cooking and maintenance shows. This was when cable was becoming a big deal, in the last couple of years. You know, the "life" channels with shows that are about how to do things. There are shows about how to do everything basically. I love them all. Cooking. On Sundays on one of those channels there are nine cooking shows in a row. Chinese, Thai, Italian, French, Indian, Mexican, Ethiopian, Vietnamese, Dutch…. It's a great time for me. Totally relaxing. And you know how I feel about wildlife shows. They're the best…. I saw one once about a snake. A fucking snake. And by the end of it I felt like I knew this snake personally. I mean, sure I knew where it lived, and what it ate, how much venom it could inject into its victims, but really I think I knew how it *felt*, what made it *tick*. That show was awesome. It changed my life. I'm sure it did. I don't know how. But I feel better than I did before I saw that show…. I mean a snake…. A snake…

from

Street Level
by Patricia Ludwick

Premiered on CBC Radio's *Morningside*, 1990, directed by Don Kowalchuk. Script available from Playwrights Guild of Canada.

• • •

"The Meaning of Money"

> *MATT Walker is 28, easy-going; he's been busking outside a liquor store in a residential area for several years to support his wife and kid. He plays a worn but decent guitar, a few coins are in the case in front of him. The tune he's strumming is a folksong (i.e. the rights are in the public domain). He tells a curious passerby how he got into busking.*

MATT

It was having a kid that got me into this, actually. See, Margo was having a hard time with the pregnancy, and I couldn't find a job for love or money. And it's coming up Christmas. Finally, one night we're sitting around sniping at each other because the cable's been cut off, you know how it is when there's no money coming in, the whole world narrows down to that one thing: money. And then it comes to me—Gordon. He's always said if I ever want to sell the axe, let him know. I don't say anything to Margo, she'll tell me not to do anything so stupid, so I just grab my coat, real casual, and head over to Gordon's. But wouldn't you know, he's not home, so I'm walking around the block to keep warm, it's December right, and I notice a bit of action outside the liquor store. There's a few people standing around laughing, and there's this old guy—he's kind of bobbing up and down, with this moth-eaten overcoat flapping around his knees. He's playing a toothcomb, and he's doing every old song you sang at camp, "You Are My Sunshine" and "The Big Rock Candy Mountain" and they're all in the same tempo, sort of jig-time, and he's doing a kind of soft-shoe step dance to it. I had a hell of a time to keep up with him. Then he hits on an old favourite of mine.

What did the blackbird say to the crow?
It ain't gonna rain no more.
Ain't gonna hail and ain't gonna snow,
Ain't gonna rain no more.

Two hours later, we're still coming up with tunes we both know, we're still laughing—and there's thirty bucks on the sidewalk in front of us. We're counting the take into his hat, and I'm trying to tell him I don't want any of it, it's his gig after all, but he starts in on this long harangue about the meaning of money. At first I think his brain's a bit addled from a lifetime of sweet wine, but after a while it starts making a weird kind of sense. The gist of it is, money isn't real. Like these coins, they don't have any value unless they're in motion—out of my pocket into your hat, out of the hat into the cash register, out of that into somebody's pay packet. But the money itself means nothing. What's real is what's happening between people, and the money is just part of that pattern of energy. You tap into that flow and the money'll just roll into your pocket on its way by. And you know. That old guy was onto something, I mean, listen, there's a million things going down at any moment, right here on the street, and they're not just random happenings, they affect each other. When you're feeling good, you're putting out something that other people pick up on and you're bound to get some of it back. Not just money—you get a smile, say, and that feeds back into the system. Right? And music wakes up other parts of the pattern of what's really going down. You catch a whiff of a tune you know and suddenly you've got this whole picture happening in your head, where you were, who you were with, what kind of day it was. Right? And for a few minutes it all comes together, like you're part of the flow, that pattern of energy. I swear to you, there's times when it feels like I'm playing the street, the music is what's holding the whole thing together. And if I could just catch hold of that tune—well, the sidewalk'd get up and dance, groceries'd be flying through the parking lot, beer would rain out of the sky— *(He laughs.)* Yeah, you think I'm as crazy as that old guy with the toothcomb, don't you? Well, I'm telling you, that tune exists all right, but you don't play it for money.

It ain't gonna rain
It ain't gonna snow,
It ain't gonna rain no more.
Come on, ev'rybody now,
Ain't gonna rain no more.

from

The Devil You Don't Know
by Joel Hynes and Sherry White

Premiered at the Resource Centre for the Arts, St. John's, 2003, directed by
Lois Brown. Script available from RCA Theatre.

• • •

> *KEITH is out on a highway somewhere in Nova Scotia,*
> *hitchhiking. He's reading a book with a flashlight...*

KEITH

One of these days when I'm old and grey I'm gonna walk into Weston's
Books up on Kenmount Road with a big bag of books. I'm gonna dump
them all out on the floor and say... "I stole every one of these books
while... that little fella right there was working."

Ever rob a book? Easiest thing in the world. Just make sure you wears
a good jacket. Hold the book in your hand and then, all in one move, this
is the key, all in one move, crouch down to a lower shelf and slide the book
up under your armpit. Grab another book of around the same size and
colour on your way back up. The clerk would have to be pretty keen or
pretty goddamn bored with their job to catch on to that one. Then you just
browse for a bit as natural as possible. You'd be surprised at the size of the
books you can get away with too. Go on then and ask 'em to locate a book
that you know they don't carry, or one that doesn't exist. "Yeah, you got
anything in by that Kavanagh fella... ahhh... Keith Kavanagh?" This helps
them feel as though they've let you down. All's left to do is to walk off
looking disappointed. Easiest thing in the world.

Oh don't get me wrong. I'm not a thief. I just think that there's different
degrees of thievery. Like that time I got picked up in Wal-Mart of all places.
Oh yeah, I swiped a copy of Pink Floyd's "The Wall." Soon as I'm out
through the door this big beefy fucker spins me around and tells me I'm
under arrest for theft. Like Roger Waters I gonna give a fuck. So I ends up
in court and it's all a big joke to everyone. The judge says "So you're a big
Pink Floyd fan Mr. Kavanagh?" All these suit and tie guys are snickering
and I says "I don't know b'y. I never got to watch the goddamn movie first

not last." S'pose I shoulda gotten a lawyer for that one. But come on, that's not stealing. From a multi-go-zillion dollar corporation like Wal-Mart? Fuck that. Stealing is when your buddy gives you twenty bucks to pick him up a gram of hash and you pinches off a nickel for yourself. That's pure thievery. Not movies or books or... liquor for that matter. So yeah, I waltzed on in to the gift shop on the ferry and robbed a bottle.

He pulls a bottle of whiskey from his bag.

So what? Wouldn't know now but the liquor corporation were gonna go under or something. What the Christ are they selling liquor in a gift shop anyhow? Ahhh, they'll never miss it. But I certainly would. Out here on the road. Oh yeah. I swiped a bunch of Nevada tickets too. That's different though. What?

KEITH puts the bottle on his face. Fade to black.

from

Dogpatch ✔
by Chaz Thorne

Premiered at the Factory Theatre, Toronto, produced by Jack in the Black
Productions, 2000.

• • •

CABBIE

Ol' Pete Power; now thur's one crazy ol' basderd. The tricks we used te play
on 'im; somethin' awful. Enyway, where wuz I…? Ernie an' me… couple
girls… up the dance—oh, yeah. Enyway, the one Ernie's with, eh? Real
mean-lookin' thing, eh? Real baddleaxe. Enyway, were all drunked up on
whisky er some craziness—Don' drink enymore, eh? Bin off the stuff nearly
four years. Docter in the army said I mighde' developed some intestinal
problems frum the stuff. Las' time I wuz drinkin' gimme the shits so bad
damn near killed me. Jesus… now whad wuz I talkin' aboat…? Shits… oh,
drinkin'. Right. So we wuz playin' tricks on ol' Pete. We'd hide 'is crutches
on 'im, an' when 'e wuz all made, hoppin' aroun' like some crazy one-legged
rabbit, lookin' fer 'is crutches, we'd trip 'im an' stuff; poor basderd. So we
geds bored a' thad an' decides wu'll ged the girls back the field, ye know.
Thinkin' they've 'ad a few so thu'll be good fer a piece a' ass, eh?

So we're up the field an' I takes the looker off te one corner, eh? An' Ernie
an' the mean-lookin' one goes off somewhere else. Enyway, 'boad a quarder
uv an hour goes by an' things is geddin' preddy hot an' heavy with the
look when I hears this loud crack, eh? An' righd afder thad I hear Ernie
screamin' bloody murder. Then, oadde' nowhere, Ernie comes runnin' by
in 'is unnerwear like 'e's bein' chased by the devil 'isself an afder 'im come
the mean-lookin' one jesd a barrellin' afder 'im in jesd 'er pan'ies with 'er
bid ol' tiddies floppin' this way an' thad… an' in 'er han' she gud this big
tree branch she pulled off uv a tree; muste' bin six feet long an' thad big
aroun'; an' wuzn' she jes' puddin' a beadin' te poor ol' Ernie with it. Turns
oad she'd fallen asleep frum the lic'er an' Ernie 'ad tried undressin' 'er an'
she come to. Well, I guess she wuzn' none too pleased aboad thad led me
tell ye; cuz she chased ol' Ernie righd inte the lake. She only didn' go afder
'im cuz she couldn' swim. I swear Ernie wuz paddlin' oad there til dawn fer

fear uv 'is life cuz the mean-lookin' one wuz standin' on shore with thad big ol' branch waidin' te bead 'is head in.... Ernie 'asn' bin back up 'ere in the Heighds te this day. Poor ol' bugger's scared te death 'e'll run inte the mean-lookin' one by accidint an' shu'll remember 'im.... Wemin're like elephants... they don' ferget...

from

Criminal Genius
by George F. Walker

Premiered at Theatre Off Park, New York, produced by Rattlestick
Productions, 1997, directed by Daniel De Raey. Script available from
Talonbooks.

• • •

PHILLIE

Hey! What's happening out there. Were those gunshots…. Well?… Well? Ah
the hell with you all… I'm sorry I ever met you…. You're just like everyone
else…. You take advantage…. You see that I'm a not-well man, that I'm
addicted to alcoholic beverages, prone to bad luck, you see that I'm not
a very strong person and you take advantage. Get me involved in something
I'm too impaired to fully understand. Whatever happens to me, I'm
blaming you. You thought you were gonna blame me, well I'm blaming
you. The forty buck thing, the shoe thing, the running thing, I'm not taking
responsibility for any of it. Who said we were bound together…. That's
crap. We're not bound. It's every man for himself. Dog eat dog. Fuck you.
Did you hear me. Fuck you? Talk about bad luck. Bad luck loves me like
I'm its mother…. Ever since I was a kid…. No. You know what? It's not
bad luck. It's people. Since I was five, six years old nothing good has ever
happened to me. I blame my parents and my teachers. I blame everyone
I ever met. Everyone…. You know if there was any justice in the world
they'll kill you all and leave me alone. But they won't. They'll kill me too.
I didn't do anything to them, okay I kicked one of them in the head, but is
that any reason to kill someone. No. Unless of course that person is me.
Sure kill me for any old reason. Who am I. No one. Nothing. Fuck all.
Phillie-Fuck-All…. You can kill him anytime you want. Kill him, fuck him,
kill him, fuck him, kill him. Who cares. He's just a pathetic asshole…. Well
isn't that a sad commentary on our society…. I mean really. I blame society
for producing that kind of callous indifference to fucked-up individuals….
I really do…. I really really do.

Long pause.

Looking back I never had a chance. My parents were idiots, my teachers were idiots, all my friends were idiots, everyone, every single person I ever met in my whole life was a mean-spirited, demented idiot. And I never complained. Never. Not once…. Not until now. I've been a fucking saint!

from

The Melville Boys
by Norm Foster

Premiered at Theatre New Brunswick, Fredericton, 1984, directed by
Malcolm Black. Script available from Playwrights Canada Press.

• • •

> *Leading up to this monologue, OWEN Melville has been told by
> his brother Lee that OWEN will never get the foreman job at the
> plant in which they both work. Previous to this, Lee has asked
> that OWEN look after his family after Lee dies. OWEN has
> adamantly refused to comply with that request.*

OWEN

I don't care what you say, and I don't care what Harvey says. I'm gonna be
the next foreman there, goddamn it. That job is gonna be mine!

> *LEE goes about picking up the beer cans.*

And you can call me a stupid son of a bitch all you want, but the fact is,
I do like working there. Yeah. And you know why? It's because… because,
when I go in there every day, I know that there's gonna be no one in there
who thinks they're better than me. No one! And if I go back to school
and get a job somewhere else, then I can't be sure it's gonna be like that,
can I? No. No, you're the one who should've done better for himself, Lee.
Not me. I belong in that plant, and I'm gonna stay in there. And I'll tell
you something else. And I mean this as a warning. If those kids of yours….
If those kids give me a hard time, they're gonna find out who's boss, and
I mean in one helluva hurry. You make sure they know that. I'm not gonna
take any crap. They do what I tell them to the first time, or else! *(turns
away from LEE, and moans)* Two little girls. Why couldn't you have boys?
I could take boys to a ball game. Teach them how to bunt. I ain't seen
a girl yet who knew how to lay down a good bunt. And I'm not gonna be
running errands for Arlene all the time either. She's a big girl. She can do
these things for herself. I'm not an errand boy. You tell her that!

from

Tales of an Urban Indian
by Darrell Dennis

Premiered at Artword Alternative, Toronto, produced by Native Earth Performing Arts, 2003, directed by Herbie Barnes. Script available from Playwrights Canada Press.

• • •

"The WASP Nest"

SIMON Douglas has been leading a double life. Despite spending most of his time on Vancouver's skid row he still manages to maintain a relationship with his WASP girlfriend Brenda. After suffering through his first meeting with Brenda's racist parents, SIMON snaps when they ask him what his plans are for their daughter.

SIMON, AGE 21

My plans? Well, I would like to marry your daughter and eventually have some children. I would have to give up acting because an artist is no father for a child to have. I'll probably get a job in a mailroom somewhere, where I can work my way up to stock boy. Oh sure it's not glamorous but at least I'll have a weekly paycheque coming in. I can invest in mutual funds, and RRSP's. If that goes well maybe I'll throw some money down on a little bungalow. I'll definitely be promoted to shipping and receiving by that time. I'll sit there at my desk, day in and day out, getting fat, losing my hair, my sex drive, my will to live. When I'm sixty-five I'll drive around the country in a Winnebago, taking pictures of portage routes and the biggest ball of twine. At nights I'll sit in my panelled den, drinking hot rum toddies, flipping back and forth between the scrambled cable channels to catch a quick glimpse of a nipple. Praying for cancer or some crippling kidney disease—anything to let me know that I'm still alive. I'll die a nobody and the only way people will know I existed will be the write-up in the obituary column that they flip past to get to the latest "Family Circus" cartoon. I will be a fine, upstanding member of the community,

suckling at the teat of so-called democracy! That sir will be my legacy!!
Then again, maybe I'll just hang around alleys, sucking cocks for crack!

from

Blovine   ✔

by Christopher Hunt

Premiered at the Joyce Doolittle Theatre at the Pumphouse Theatres, Calgary, 2001, directed by Sean Bowie. From the script *CockTales*, available from Ground Zero Theatre.

. . .

> *FARMBOY is an actor of any age (mid 20s on up), and his costume would have a rural feel if desired. (e.g. denim overalls and workboots) No set is required, but a bit of "Deliverance" inspired banjo music might be used as an intro.*

FARMBOY

Growing up on the farm was a blessing and a curse as far as me and my cock were concerned. On the one hand, sex was everywhere—on the other hand, it was all animals—I was a virgin until I was 21. But there's a point in every boy/man's life where you have a perma-woody and are looking for inspiration, guidance and relief.

Of course my parents were there, so there MUST have been human sex, but I never saw or heard anything. I did once catch my dad lingering a tad too long in the bras and panties section of the Sears Catalogue, but that's about it. Even with two older brothers, I have no memory of vicarious action. And my far younger sister wasn't any help until her friends got breasts, by which time I was almost in university.

That left the animals. And we didn't have sheep. There were cattle, some horses, a few chickens and an assortment of cats and dogs. Not much action to be got there, except by watching. Horses seemed to have huge Slinky-sized members—thick as soup cans. Kinda slow and lazy to get aroused, I thought. The bulls, by contrast, were much thinner—they seemed like the size of my thumb, but much longer—like a bloody yardstick!—and they seemed to get erect instantly. Like a sword unsheathed. I always feared that one of the bulls would accidentally break it mid-mount, but I don't remember that happening. THIS is what

I remember. Here's the story of my first bold steps into the animal kingdom.

It was during one of those hot and horny phases (that still happen, thankfully) when everything reminded me of sex. I was milking a cow (no, I'm not gonna have sex with the cow), thinking of girls in school, getting a stiffy, when I spy the heifer calf in the pen across the aisle in the barn. It's the calf of the cow I'm milking, and one of my chores is to feed it some of the milk and take the rest up to the house. It's quite a small calf, recently taken from mommy, so they have these special pails to feed calves milk with. It's a metal pail with a stiff rubber nipple on the bottom that the calf sucks on like a surrogate mother (you can probably see where this is going…). I'd always thought that this nipple-thing was about the same length and thickness as an erect adult penis would be—in hindsight, I think I was being generous. Now these calves are cute and soft and friendly. I'd played with them and been licked by their soft yet rough tongues for years, but I'd never really looked at them in THAT way, if you know what I mean. But I was desperate. And the thought of that warm, slobbery tongue sucking me off was powerful stuff, and the tiny bulge in my overalls prompted me into action.

So, after finishing the milking, I made sure the coast was clear of humans (I'd never live it down if my brothers, or my dad, or God forbid my MOM caught sight of THIS). I then got into the pen with the calf and teased it with the nipple pail to let it know what was coming (hopefully), then threw the pail over the fence, unzipped my overalls and whipped out my own surrogate suckable. The calf was momentarily confused, but hunger (and perhaps the similarly shaped—though somewhat smaller—object between my legs) soon had it licking and slurping.

It all happened so quickly, though not quickly enough. At first, it actually felt good—I mean, here was a young soft living thing eagerly lapping at my impending manhood. But I hadn't counted on the rambunctiousness and hunger of this little bovine. I'm not sure if you've ever seen a calf suckle (either from its mother or from a nipple pail), but when they get impatient, or if the milk isn't coming fast enough, they tend to butt their heads—this is often accompanied by a yanking of the nipple. So, apparently my milk wasn't coming fast enough.

My first "no" feeling was when the calf gave me a head butt. Man, that hurt! I pulled back, but the calf was hungry—the next sensation was a searing

pain as she bit and tugged on my knob. Now THAT hurt like STINK! *I'd*
had enough—I had to get out of there. Trouble was, the calf needed to be
fed—she kept butting and then yanking—my back to the barn wall—her
sandpaper tongue—butting and yanking—the mixed smell of hay, fresh
milk and manure—a yank, a butt…

I had put my cock in the mouth of a hungry animal—what the HELL was
I thinking?! It was all I could do to get my cock out of her mouth and back
in my pants. I'm fine—really—I'm fine. No blood, no scars, no therapy. But
from then on, anytime I got near that calf, she went crazy for my crotch.
I was paranoid that my brothers and my dad would see this and *know* what
I'd done. Had they done it at my age? Why didn't they warn me? Was this
some absurd rural rite of passage? So despite the embarrassing nudgings
from my little acquaintance, I was having none of it. As far as I was
concerned, it was over between us. I'd learned my lesson. Oh yeah—
I learned my lesson.

from

Snake in Fridge
by Brad Fraser

Premiered at the Royal Exchange Theatre, Manchester, England, 2000, directed by Braham Murray. Script available from NeWest Press.

• • •

> *TRAVIS, a young black man, is sharing a haunted house with his psychotic, bodybuilder best friend and a number of other young people working on the fringes of the sex industry. There are many strange things happening in the house and they've began to spill over into TRAVIS's life, as evidenced by this incident he relates to his roommates.*

TRAVIS

So. I'm in the Bank of Nova Scotia just over on Yonge and Carlton making a payment on my million-dollar student loan for that fucking arts degree that got me a job as a busboy. This nice Filipino lady is helping me. Next to me there's a big bald white guy being waited on by a Korean guy. Past them there's an Indian woman being waited on by this Twinkie guy with red hair. On the other corner of the counter there's a Hispanic teller—female—with a fat blonde chick in short shorts and a pop-top. Right in the centre of all this is a black woman at a desk kinda presiding over everything. The fat blonde chick and the Hispanic woman are having some kinda argument. Something about a lost card or something. Everyone's listening and pretending not to. The fat chick's getting more and more irate. I'm a good customer at this bank. I'm not going back to my branch. Give me a card now blah blah blah. The black woman who's been listening to all of this finally says, I'm sorry, but without valid ID we can't issue you a new bank card firmly but nicely. The fat chick screams, You can't do this to me, you'll be so sorry and struts away. Everyone's like Whew glad that socially embarrassing moment is over. Then just as the fat chick is nearly out the door she says in this real slippery voice Nigger Bitch. For a second I have no idea what she said. It's like hearing a phrase in another language that sounds familiar y'know? Then it hits me. I have to say something. I can't just let her walk out of here but it's like my brain's frozen or something.

Then my mouth opens and without even knowing it I say Fuck you you fat dump-eating honky cunt! Immediately I sense this is not the appropriate response. The bad white guy beside me says Good comeback you jig cocksucker. The Filipino lady says Leave him alone you pasty Nazi bastard. The Korean who obviously has issue with the gal says Shut up you stupid yellow hag. The Twinkie teller slams his cash drawer shut and says You goddamn third world gooks can't talk this way in a bank. The Indian woman smacks her hand on the counter and screams Just get me my fucking money you nelly fudgepacker! Then this Hispanic woman says something like Shut up you Paki cow in Spanish. Someone keeps screaming Kike kike! and I don't think there are even like any Jews in the bank. The black woman jumps up from her desk, screams, Call me a nigger bitch you flabby cooze and takes off after the fat chick who is trying to beat it out the door. Everyone's yelling. People are throwing things. The Hispanic woman's trying to hold the black woman back and security's holding the fat white chick. It was a fucking race riot in the middle of the Bank of Nova Scotia. I bolted fast. But that's not the fucked-up thing. No. What's fucked up is that I still had to make a goddamn four-hundred-dollar student loan payment for an education that apparently taught me nothing. Where'd the big fucking TV come from?

from

The Adventures of a Black Girl in Search of God
by Djanet Sears

Premiered at the duMaurier Theatre, Toronto, produced by Obsidian Theatre Company and Nightwood Theatre, 2002, directed by Djanet Sears. Script available from Playwrights Canada Press.

• • •

> *The small church is packed. The desecration of the church has brought everyone out. MICHAEL stands in front of the congregation without his church robe and delivers what might be the most powerful words he's ever spoken from that pulpit.*

MICHAEL

"This kind of thing never happens here."

That's what they think. That's what we think. "Everything is fine here in this country." We've grown so comfortable that we believe racism, no, white supremacy is a phenomenon that only happens south of the border. Well folks, we live in the south of the north. That they could do this to God's house…. And we will not take those hideous and repugnant words down. We will not whitewash the truth of our situation. We will leave this desecration in place as a reminder. Because this is all about our attempts to upturn the Holland Township council decision to change the name of Negro Creek Road, you know that. This is our home. And these threats…. This racial intimidation will not deter us in the least from our cause. We are a steadfast people. It is this characteristic in us that has helped us survive the most severe and vicious atrocities. Our forebears survived so that we may breathe the air we breathe at this very moment. They can try to put fear in us. They can even burn us down. But we will continue to fight for our right to take up space on this earth. See you at the march tomorrow.

from

Patience
by Jason Sherman

Premiered at the Tarragon Theatre, Toronto, 1998, directed by Ian Prinsloo. Script available from Playwrights Canada Press.

• • •

"All Aboard"

Two old friends; a chance encounter; the revelation of an epiphany.

PAUL

I tell you. I see kids on the street where I never used to see them. I feel sorry for them, I do. In my mind, I comfort them, I reach out to them. But then I walk past them, and as I walk by, I feel fear and hatred. I see a woman begging for money where there never used to be women begging; I think to give her money, but I cross the street to avoid her. Why is that? I tell you. I always thought I was on the side of the good. But I know now, I never was. I was on the side of the strong, of the selfish. Yes, and when I accepted that, when I accepted what I am, then was I able to take back my life. You see? "Good" and "bad," they have no meaning. The lion kills the deer for food; we weep for the deer but the lion must eat. You see? The beggar woman and the hungry children, the lost and the weak, the near dead and the barely living, their age and shit, their smells and looks, these are things which must be if you and I are to have all that we have. What would you do if you lost everything you had? If your business were to fail? Your wife should leave you? If you were never to see your children again? We coast, we coast. And if one day, everything that defines you were to vanish, what would you have left? I didn't wait to find out, you see. I knew I was unhappy, and I can see, I can see that you are, too. You don't like what you've become, Reuben. You wake up and there are things which must be done. You do them, but you feel nothing. Your senses are dulled, your mind's gone numb. You think about death and you're afraid. Because you know you're dying. Every day is not one more day of your life, it's one less. One less. One less. Think about this, Reuben. You have everything you need. But do you need everything you have?

from

Habitat
by Judith Thompson

Premiered at the Bluma Appel Theatre, Toronto, 2001, directed by
Katherine Kaszas. Script available from Playwrights Canada Press.

• • •

> *LEWIS defends his actions and his motives to the people of*
> *Mapleview Lanes, the neighbourhood where he has opened*
> *a group home for troubled teens.*

LEWIS

Hell, I'll admit everything. Sometimes, you know what? If there's some
money left after the kids have everything they need and the new wiring and
the copper plumbing is paid for and the roof and their teeth yes, sometimes
I borrow some of that money, throw it into one of mybusinesses, or loan
it to my mother, or one of my sisters, if she doesn't have enough to feed
her kids till her next welfare cheque and I shouldn't do that, even though
I always pay it back eventually, I guess I shouldn't; but who among you
has not done that with your taxes or business profits or whatever, eh? Eh?
And yes I don't want any surprises here today, I had in a way… an…
unconsummated—a silent—love affair with one of my wards… with
Sparkle here; sounds like a crazy thing to say, but I want to be totally
perfectly honest here, I have felt—desire for this young man, I have looked
at him I have even fantasized about him, alone in my bed; dirty thoughts;
he is eighteen, true, but anyway, it's still wrong, wrong wrong wrong, it's
monstrous—to even think the thought and I am not going to stand here
tellin you to be saints, to do what is right what is true what is just when
I am corroding at the edges myself. Oh yeah, I'm gay, does that scare ya?
So, yeah, I crossed a couple of lines I shouldn't have, and I regret it. I will
regret it till the day I die. But I'll tell ya, they will not be crossed ever again;
I would do anything for these kids, you know that? I would honestly give
my life. So. What are you going to do about it, are you going to throw me
out?

He looks at Margaret, walks to her, kneels down.

You. Here. You are Mapleview Lanes, you created it, you represent it, you are a fine and thinking person with a conscience, I think, and I am in your hands. If you tell me to go, I will go. And if you want me to stay, I'll stay.

from

Bag Babies
by Allan Stratton

Premiered at Theatre Passe Muraille, Toronto, 1990, directed by John Bourgeois. Script available from Playwrights Canada Press.

• • •

> *ELGIN Marbles is an insane, billionaire monster, who has built a fortune exploiting the poor, while posing as a philanthropist. In this monologue, to interviewer Katie Hughes, Marbles sings the praises of his methods, beginning with his venture to rid society of street drugs.*

ELGIN

(to KATIE) My solution to street drugs? The Elgin Marbles Haven of Hope: an island I bought in the middle of the ocean. I give junkies a one-way ticket. They're gone, crime's down and I convert the crack houses to condos. Why do they go, you ask? Free Drugs! I say, "Welcome. Open the orifice of your choice. Pig out. Go nuts." The best part? There's no cost! I hand out the overruns from my Marbles Pharmaceutical Corp. Consider it a drug recycling program. Conservation: watchword of the millennium. And I give 'em hobbies. Yes sir. I get 'em higher than kites then put 'em behind sewing machines. Miles and miles of sewing machines. With colourful fabrics. They go crazy. *(He does a frenzied impersonation of a speed freak on a sewing machine.)* Bdrdrdrdr. Bdrdrdrdr. Bdrdrdrdr. Bingo! Designer clothes with the Marbles label! They screw up on an item, no prob. I donate it to the Marbles-Hand-Me-Downs for the Poor. Great tax deduction. Let's hear it for free enterprise! Whooppee! The trouble today is—nobody thinks. Look at our prisons. A captive workforce! A license to print money! WE GOTTA PRIVATIZE OUR PRISONS! MAKE 'EM WORK! I'm not talking chain gangs, neither. No sir, I'm talking "rehab through manual job skills." I'll contract 'em to my Marbles Foundation to build libraries, galleries and clinics. The taxpayers save. Society's enriched. I make a mint. And those little buggers'll get more exercise than they'll know what to do with! You wanna call it slavery? Wake up and smell the coffee. We keep the Third World in economic slavery and who gives

a bucket of warm spit. Nobody. Why? Cuz we like bargains, that's why! AND YOU CAN'T BEAT SWEATSHOPS FOR COMPETITIVE PRICES! Face reality: Slavery is capitalism with balls!

from

Home is My Road
by Florence Gibson

Premiered at the Factory Theatre, Toronto, 2003, directed by Ken Gass. Script available from Playwrights Canada Press.

• • •

> *CLAUDE, a Romanian baby broker who is selling babies to westerners in the aftermath of the revolution in 1993, is in this scene with his henchman, Dumptruck, putting the screws to Stefan, a young impoverished Roma (Gypsy). Dumptruck has just levelled Stefan and CLAUDE is now telling him to find some destitute Roma women whom he can force to sell their babies on the black market.*

CLAUDE

You know I used to be a member of the party. But now I think, communism, capitalism, what does it matter? Either way, the big heavy guys are held upon the shoulders of the weaklings—structurally unsound systems from the ground up, you could say. And I feel that weight Stefan, same as you. We're bugs, squashed bugs. Under communism we were the ants, going along the trail, carrying many times our weight for the sake of the colony, and where did that get us? Fuck communism. Fuck the ants. Turn into a cockroach and live in the cracks between the assholes.

The point being, Stefan, look up.

> *Pries STEFAN's chin with his boot.*

Look up to me when I'm speaking to you.
I want my pound of flesh. Or seven, or eight pounds.

> *STEFAN stares at him.*

Healthy, white, and no diseases too.

> *CLAUDE laughs.*

What am I talking about. He doesn't know what I'm talking about.

DUMPTRUCK laughs.

Stefan. I've got mothers waiting for babies, and no storks to deliver them.

STEFAN tries to go. DUMPTRUCK stops him.

Western women, big bundles of nerves, so uptight, how do their husbands ever fuck them? We are obliged to help them, you and I.

And your people Stefan, we help them too, we offer the best solution to an insoluble problem. We set the children free, like birds, and one day they will come back, they will bring the gifts of the west, and they will heal us.

DUMPTRUCK pins STEFAN.

You want to be like Dumptruck?—He goes to Istanbul, he sells his kidney! Go on, show him your scar.

DUMPTRUCK is ashamed, and won't.

Your little kumpania is such a burden for you.
And Trinquet. Your beautiful sister Trinquet.
How will she survive if you go to jail? Her situation is so, severe, and yet—.
When she says she loves me, what am I to believe? Is her love a public truth, and a private lie? Is it a tortuous beauty, like her own? Is it any different for me now, now her husband hasn't been heard from in months? What could have happened to her man, a man who used to talk so much, for him to be
so
silent?

DUMPTRUCK tightens his hold on STEFAN.

Who was he? Stefan. Nobody. Nothing. Gypsy.
You work your magic on the mothers Stefan. You speak to them, you make them see... your choice, Stefan.

from

Skate It Off, Bobby
by T. Berto

Premiered at the George Luscombe Theatre, Guelph, 2001, directed by Lucas Raymond. Script available from the playwright at aberto@uoguelph.ca.

• • •

> *The action takes place in the bedroom. Carl and GIANNI, in their thirties, are romantically involved but have great difficulty moving forward because Carl is a survivor of sexual abuse. GIANNI is a refugee from Pinochet's Chile—where he lost both his parents in the coup. Their struggle comes to a head when Carl refuses to progress their relationship—sexually. After physically forcing Carl not to walk away from him and pinning him to the bed, Carl retorts that GIANNI can't possibly compare "just coming through a revolution" with the horrors of Carl's abuse. GIANNI finally tells his own story.*

GIANNI

> *Struggling to stay calm. Over the course of the monologue GIANNI slowly releases Carl.*

I…I…I remember…
You know when I think about it, it's like I had a fever, the kind that you had when you're that old. It's blurred, but like… the feel of the sheets or what you smelled always stays. I remember smelling sugar on the stove—Marta had burned something. I was sleepy… I'd heard the pops coming in the window, all the night before. Papa had come in and said not to worry. But it was Papa that came in. He was home that morning. In his suit. Jesus!

> *He moves off from Carl and struggles to conjure up the images.*

When the trucks came they took everybody. Even Marta, our cook. The whole street was emptied. There were soldiers, but everyone just lined up. Everyone was so quiet. I… asked what was happening and Papa looked at me hard to I didn't ask again. Mama wouldn't look at me. They drove us into the stadium. That was where we would get to play one day, if we were really good, they said in school. It was so big. So full with people. It was then that people started to get scared. My... Mama held me so hard that it hurt. There was an old woman getting out that was having trouble. This soldier went up to her, to like help her down, but instead he just grabbed her by the arm and yanked her down. She fell on her face and everyone just, got sorta tight and... clenched. The woman got up and just wept quietly. The soldiers all had eyes like hard black marbles.

We just stood and watched the trucks and buses come. There were so many. Everyone had the same look on their face when they stepped down. The... whole stadium was filling up with fright. If people stumbled or got pushed they made no sound. But there were children starting to scream.

Then this man came down from one of the buses. I can still see his face... one of the soldiers smiled at him and moved his hands as if he was playing a guitar and the man nodded. He took him over to the truck in the middle—where all the soldiers were. There was a guitar there. You could tell he was a famous man and it seemed, that he was needed to play something, anything so the people would calm down. When he got on top of the truck the soldiers grabbed and held out his hands. They took a hammer and smashed his hand. When he didn't scream they smashed the other one. They pushed a guitar into him and yelled, "Now play us a song." I must have been far from him but it seemed like I was right beside him.

My mother then put me down. Everyone was starting to scream. She grabbed my face and looked right into it. She said so serious. "You're Marta's, our cook, her son. You're six years old." But "I'm ten" I kept thinking. Who could think I'm six? But I didn't say anything. She then told me to go over to a group of children with their mothers. The children were screaming. I started to go over and then wanted to go back—the babies made so much noise. When I turned around to go back I couldn't see where my mother was anymore. I started to cry. A woman grabbed me and pulled me over to the wall and told me to hush or she would hit me. Then the man, the man with smashed hands came and fell on his knees in front of all the people.

And... he started to sing, very badly and quietly, a song. Everyone knew the song. People started singing. It seemed everything went quiet except for singing now. The soldiers began to move all over like insects, with their shiny black metal.

Then they went up to those singing loudest, right in front of the smashed hands and just started spraying them with their guns. That's how it started. I was ten. That was old enough for some of the soldiers, some of the bad men. I though I was so old then. But I guess, just a boy. So.

Yes, I "came through a revolution." And you can't even begin to imagine what.... You! You got diddled a bit as a teenager. Well boo-fucking-hoo. Can you walk? Can you hold down a job? Can you go to movies? Can you have holidays? Can you speak to strangers? Can you sleep at night without all sorts of pills? Are your testicles whole? Do you have scars from electric wires all over your body? Can you call up your mum and dad and ask if you had the German measles? Don't you tell me about horror!

> *Beat.*

I think I am okay. I came through real... light. I've got some relatives and live in a nice society. Have you seen people killed in front of...

No. I am okay. You worry about a man who took away innocence. He's probably lonely and dying of drink somewhere. What about my... what about the people that took all liberty, freedom, dignity, body and soul, life and family from me... from my... what about that? And all for a few pennies less an hour that they'd have to pay them! And they're, and they're still... fucking still... wining and dining on the profits made from those they stepped on. Living like kings in a home we can never go back to. I'm sorry. I have difficulty with the... the problems... that plague you. You still have almost everything. I am okay. You should be.

from

Mourning Dove
by Emil Sher

Premiered at the Great Canadian Theatre Company, Ottawa, 2005, directed by Lorne Pardy. Script available from Playwrights Canada Press.

• • •

> *DOUG Ramsay's severely disabled daughter Tina has endured twelve years of constant pain. While his wife Sandra has pinned her hopes that a major operation is for the best, both acknowledge little can be done to alleviate their daughter's suffering. DOUG has decided to take Tina's life, and in a last desperate attempt to understand her pain he asks Keith— a developmentally handicapped friend—to tie him up. On DOUG's orders Keith is to leave the shed where DOUG lies bound in knots, and return a few hours later. Instead, Sandra appears a few moments later to relay a phone message. She unties DOUG, and insists no one can understand their daughter's pain. DOUG is determined to try.*

DOUG

Cut out my tongue so I can't speak. *(beat)* Twist my muscles into impossible knots. Twist them the way I've seen you wring a mop. Real tight. *(beat)* Drill holes in my back. Drill like my back was a sheet of plywood. If you hit a nerve, keep drilling, like you're drilling for oil, like you're drilling your way to the ends of the earth and won't stop until you get there. *(beat)* Saw off my thighbone. Saw it right off. Take the sawed off part and shove it back into the hip socket. It won't fit, 'cause you've sawed off the ball part. C'mon. Shove that cut-off bone into the socket where it belongs. *(beat)* Stick a feeding tube in me. You heard what Kovacs said. Chances are good I'm going to lose even more weight. Thirty-eight pounds and dropping. Get that feeding tube into me. A tube for every hole in my body while you're at it…. It won't stop. You heard Kovacs. It will not stop. More operations. More "intervention." *(beat)* When you're finished. When you've finished all your cutting and drilling and sawing, send in my parents. My parents, they love me. God, yes. Their love, it's like my daily seizures. It's a sure thing. Thing is, it's not enough. *(beat)* My pain is greater than my parent's love. *(beat)* No more. *(beat)* No more.

from

Blowfish
by Vern Thiessen

Premiered at Commerce Place, Edmonton, co-produced by Northern Light Theatre and the National Arts Centre, 1996, directed by D.D. Kugler. Script available from Playwrights Canada Press.

• • •

LUMIERE the caterer has invited the audience to a banquet. During the course of the meal, he tells his guests stories that appear, at first, unconnected, but soon become very personal to his life. Here is one such story.

LUMIERE

Once upon a time, there was a young boy who lived in a small to medium-sized home, in a small to medium-sized city, in a western province, in a place known as Canada. Every evening, the boy's mother carefully created dinner to the rhythm of the boy's father turning the pages of his newspaper.

One evening, the family sat down and dug into large helpings of scalloped potatoes, fresh carrots from the garden, and roast chicken. As the young boy picked up a drumstick, he could not believe his incredible luck. While the parents used cutlery to wrestle with their thighs and breasts, the young son said: "Look Mom, look Dad, I don't need a knife and fork. I've got meat with a handle."

A pause descended on the table. The young son thought this natural, that meat came with or without handles. The boy's twin laughed, and even the mother could not suppress a smile. The father, however, stood up, and without finishing dinner said: "Come with me."

Father and son travelled in silence. The son feared that he had said something terribly wrong, wondering: "Where is Dad taking me?"

Father and son entered a shop.

"Wait here."

The boy did as he was told, taking in the dimly lit surroundings, and plugging his nose against the overwhelming smell of... something. He wasn't quite sure what it was, but the smell was strong, and made his tummy turn.

The father returned with a man.

"Come 'ere," said the man. The boy, holding his father's hand, followed the man down a long tunnel and through a door. The boy could not believe his eyes: In front of him lay a room filled with animals. Sides of beef, legs of lamb, and fresh fowl. All of them dead.

"Come 'ere."

The father nudged his son, who stepped forward, the knot in his stomach growing. The man took a chicken, freshly plucked, and put it onto a cutting board.

"This is an animal. This is meat. It was once alive, and now it is dead."

With that, the man brought down the blade hard. The boy felt the knot in his stomach grow tighter. The man quickly and efficiently gutted the bird, letting the insides stream out.

The son watched the blood ooze, he saw the chicken's eye look dark and dead, he had visions of his own death, felt the blood drain from his face, and as the smell of innards reached the sensitive nerves of the young boy's nose, he leaned over and threw up on the butcher.

And so a mother's meal was wasted.

But a valuable lesson was learned.

from

My Mother's Feet
by Gina Wilkinson

Premiered at the Berkeley Street Theatre, Toronto, produced by the
Canadian Stage Company, 2005, directed by Micheline Chevrier. Script
available from Great North Artists Management.

• • •

> *DAN (late thirties) tells a frightening story about his young son
> playing alone in the back yard. Until the last possible moment
> the audience must believe that the unsupervised child has
> actually drowned; only then do we realize that DAN's real terror
> stems from the discovery of a mysterious person watching the
> tiny, naked boy over the garden fence.*

DAN

(to us; defensive) It wasn't my fault!

He was alone in the yard. He asked to me to fill up his wading pool—
I didn't have time. *(imitating his son)* "Come on, Dad! Let's do Force of
Evil!" That's his game. He wraps his arms in long strips of saran wrap. This,
so I am told, protects him from The Debilitating Psychic Rays of the Evil
Force. "You are banished, Evil Force!" *(smiles)* He also carries around a big
old magnifying glass that used to be mine. He holds it in front of him,
traps the light and blinds the unsuspecting. I love to watch him, as he
makes his way through his own private world. Facing down monsters,
overcoming all odds, shooting rays of pure light into the darkness. A lot
of the time he just slaughters ants with the magnifying glass. Or blasts the
squirrels with his super-soaker. *(suddenly defensive)* It's a fenced-in yard!
A high fence! He's quite safe! I built my studio in the second floor sunroom
overlooking the back garden just so I can keep an eye on him! *(beat)* He's
always changing. Day to day. Perceptibly. Sometimes at dinner I look at him
and his features have moved—shifted—just since breakfast. He is liquid. He
takes a new shape right in front of my eyes. I don't want to miss any of it.
"Stop looking at me, Dad! You're staring at me again!" I know I am. I can't
help myself. *(forcing himself to get back to the story)* It was really hot
yesterday. The first whiff of the scorching to come. I kept breaking things.

I'm making this model for a theatre set. It's a musical production of *Goldilocks*. I'd snapped the legs of the baby bear chair for the third time, and I was cursing and I... I happened to glance up! I just happened to look out the window, down into the yard, and... there he was... lying face down in the water.

(agitated) I never leave him alone! Never!

The pool was in the centre of the lawn—it is a toddler's pool, but he's still short enough to lie full out in it. Submerge himself completely. *(pleading)* I was working—I didn't see it happen!

He must've found the foot pump in the basement, and blown it up on his own. Now that's a job! That takes me at least twenty minutes. I hadn't looked up for twenty minutes! He must've dragged the garden hose out from the breezeway—it's heavy that coil!—lugged it out on his narrow shoulders, turned the water on and waited for it to fill. That takes time! It's amazing how much water that little pool holds. That's another twenty minutes. At least! Forty minutes I wasn't watching. Forty minutes I had missed! *(quiet)* He didn't have any pants on.... He's always taking off his pants. He says they feel crispy against his skin. *(beat; quiet)* His body was floating. His arms spread, his big t-shirt ballooning out around his thin frame, his little bum a glowing white button against the blue bottom of the pool. Face down and still. A twig on the surface of the water. *(adrenaline pumping in him)* I rise up from my chair like I'm coming out of freezing. I blink, blink—trying to adjust from the inside shadow to the bright outside, and—before it bursts—the scream mounting in my lungs.... Before I can hurl myself down the stairs and out the back door.... Before my heart can club its way out of my chest.... He flips over. He flips, like a plastic buoy held under popping up. *(laughing)* Water spraying from his mouth, his skinny legs kicking and thrashing. And he's whooping and shrieking, sending arcs of water up into the sunshine! Up, up, up! I follow the drops of rainbow! A cascade of crystal rising up, up, up... to the top of the fence behind him! *(He stops. He isn't laughing any more.)* And there I stop.

As the diamond shower returns to the grass... I stop. *(grim)* At a pair of eyes. Looking over. Over my fence.

from

The Lost Boys ✔
by R.H. Thomson

Premiered at the Great Canadian Theatre Company, Ottawa, 2001, directed by Jonas Jurasas. Script available from Playwrights Canada Press.

. . .

"Witness"

The "Man" in The Lost Boys *has challenged himself to see how far back he can retrace the last steps of his four great uncles who never survived the First World War. As he parses the pencilled omissions in his great uncles' war letters and wanders the mud of the former battlefields at night, he asks why? Why retrace? Why go back? Why look at all?*

ACTOR

My father was killed in a car accident. His station wagon left the road and rolled and rolled. He was alone. The road was absolutely straight. There was no other traffic. He died away from us all and we didn't see his body until four days after at the funeral home. After the funeral I knew I had to find it. I had to find the place. Using the police report I drove that section of Ontario highway. At each straightaway, I would get out and look for signs… tire marks, disturbances, I wasn't sure what exactly. Nothing. I would find nothing and move on, nothing again or perhaps I thought just marks in my imagination. I felt my father slipping even further away. Standing by the roadside everything was questioned, even my reason for the search. After an hour or so, I really can't remember what time, on a very long straight stretch, I saw what I thought was a disturbance in the gravel. I got out. There were two distinct signs leading slowly off, over the edge and down into a wide, grassy ditch. I descended, I was confused and excited. I had no idea what I would look for. But there, lying right across the marks coming down the grass bank, was a long indentation. Was it the length of a station wagon? In disbelief I find embedded in the earth pieces of plastic and glass, what I presumed was a side mirror from my father's car. I knew from the report that it had rolled many times. I found a second horizontal gash, grass beaten down. Again debris embedded in the earth.

Again I followed and again I found a third. What do I want to find? Why am I here? More pieces of car, this time... glass, bits of grill... and this time I'm certain because I pick out of the earth a station wagon's logo. I'm hearing sounds now. Seeing the distance between the impacts, passenger side, driver's side, passenger side, I can hear the noise and the violent clutter of the last seconds of my father's life. At first I know he was within the spinning vehicle. But I also know that in the end he was thrown free. I used what remained of my logic to imagine the last arc. Six metres away I found a small area of depressed grass. I knelt. This couldn't be where he lay... where officers stood... where a stretcher was brought... where medics' fingers pressed and listened? I press my hands to the earth. What am I going to feel, my father's body? There pressed deep was a part of his glasses, the left half, dirt smearing the lens. I know they were his and his only because still attached was a piece of sailor's twine which he used to hang them round his neck. A neck which I knew at that moment to be broken.

I've come as far as I can. I am as close to him in his last instant that I can be. I have placed my feet in his footsteps, to know him, to be there, to be here. That's all I can do. Witness.

from

My Father's Penis
by Daniel Libman

Premiered at the Joyce Doolittle Theatre at the Pumphouse Theatres, Calgary, 2001, directed by Sean Bowie. From the script *CockTales*, available from Ground Zero Theatre.

• • •

> *A middle-aged ARCHITECT muses on how perspective changes everything: in architecture… and in life, as he deals with the reality of his father's death.*

ARCHITECT

I am home. My parents' home. I am an adult. Home to visit my father. Who is dying of cancer.

My father. Who was strong. And wise. And reliable…

…is maybe 80 pounds. He is in pain, but under control with morphine. He is lucid, and relatively speaking, comfortable.

But with two weeks left to live, he is approaching incontinence. No big deal. As the body weakens, the ability to even warn us that he needs the bottle to pee is diminishing, and diminishing rapidly.

But with two weeks to go he can still say in a whisper, "peeee…." So the nurse gone, my mother busy, there is no one but me on my first hour back home to help him. A moment of panic and the bottle is found, another moment of panic as his sheet is drawn back. I pull back his now seemingly huge and baggy underwear and position the bottle and take hold of…
I take hold of…

Jesus… I am holding my father's penis.

"You don't touch another guy's penis." Memory of my father's old warning hits me anew.

I never have. Before. I feel somewhat an expert on penises, or at least *my* penis. At that moment, I realize my expertise…. Well, my research is relatively…. The sample has been a small one, no pun intended. The control group nonexistent. But I am touching my father's penis, and I have only one thought in my head.

"I am touching my father's penis." This is the first penis I have ever touched that was not attached to my body. I have no idea why it should matter. I can only confess that it does.

It is yellowish, but otherwise... *exactly as it was when I first saw it.* "This... helped... give... me... life."

My father, seemingly less concerned, be it the need, be it the morphine, be it discomfort.... My father pees.

He... *pees.* Fills the bottle. "Good on ya Dad," I cheer to myself. Somewhat of a novice on the bottle, I only drip a tiny bit. My father, relieved, is also... relieved. His son has helped him pee, and he is okay with it. Or at least: He has no choice. But he can whisper and I lean in and he says "Thanks."

I knew he wasn't gonna say "Don't touch another guy's penis" but still...

Within a week, he can no longer really communicate. Or he can, but the effort is huge and the effect negligible. Nods and waves and little tiny noises for sips of water, but the battle to control his bladder has been surrendered to greater doses of morphine. He is... incontinent.

The nurse tapes a kind of tube to my dad's penis. I watch and feel revulsion. I feel shame. I feel the end is nigh. I knew it was, but now my father's penis is not doing his bidding. It has abandoned him, or simply given up the fight. I am mad at my father's penis. But I am really only scared.

I am scared of death. I am scared of *his* death. I am scared of a preview of my own. The thing that gave me life, is dying...

I fear the aloneness, for he is completely withdrawn now. There but not, breathing but just, sentient but mute. And neutered. By the cancer, by the morphine.

He is leaving, he is dying, and the thing that said most "man" is taped and subdued and held and wrapped and...

His breathing intensifies. I hold his hand.

The breathing, more and more shallow, more and more laboured, more and more and more, faster and faster and faster...

And then a pause.... Then a little more rapid breathing...

And another pause.... A tiny bit more rapid breathing...

The pattern is unmistakable. The reverse pattern of birth, a pale imitation of ecstasy, the true rhythm of...

But it is *not* a pause... but an end. *The* end. Because there *is* no more breathing. It does not start again. It is, was, the true rhythm of... *death.*

I go to the bathroom. There were several unbroken hours of vigil, of life and death, moments profound and now... this. The bathroom.

Now everything has changed. And nothing. Nothing *has.* Changed. I am there. Like before. I stand before the toilet to pee and glance up.

There, in the mirror, unmistakable in the harsh light of the bathroom, there above the toilet...?

I squint to refocus my eyes, but here it is... conspicuous, indisputable, undeniable, only... from an entirely new perspective:

(pause) My father's penis.

(looking down, then looking up) Mine.

from

Fathers and Sons
by Don Hannah

Premiered at the Tarragon Theatre, Toronto, 1998, directed by Don Hannah. Script available from Dundurn Press.

• • •

"Giver and Receiver Meet"

In this play about the lifelong relationship between a father and his son, ALLEN, the son has been helping his mother move into a retirement home.

ALLEN

Helena and Elizabeth go back to Toronto and I stay on at the old house. Bobby and his wife arrive and we get started. Mom tries to help, tries to be delighted when we show her things that none of us have seen for years. A doll from her childhood, Bobby's teddy bear, Dad's masonic apron. We work for days. Packing things she will take to her seniors' apartment, sorting out which things are for yard sale, which for auction.

Tucked away in an old strongbox are the things my father could never throw away. Some old photos, a ration book from the war, an old masonic badge. There is a stack of all the birthday and Father's Day cards that we ever gave him. One of them I remember from primary school: faded brown construction paper, rounded corners—it's supposed to look like a wallet and has red yarn threaded through the holes I carefully punched around the edges.

Inside my greeting card wallet is the first poem I every wrote:

"Roses are red
Poppies are too
You are my father
Happy Father's Day to you"

The construction paper takes me back to Miss Rodd's classroom, to the way I would order my desktop: pencils in the wooden groove, scissors and eraser beside them, glue in the old inkwell hole in the upper right corner.

I remember sitting at my desk feeling the way that I imagined Dad felt sitting at his desk at the office: filled with accomplishment and importance, a king of business.

I remember my father coming home after work—remembering waiting on the front steps for Bert Seaman's big car to pull up.

I remember going for walks with my father, remember Dad holding my hand while we drop sticks into a ditch swollen with fast moving water. "Careful, careful," he said—he always seemed to be telling me to be careful. When he told me that there was so much water because of heavy snows melting in the woods above the town, it was more than information: the connection between deep snow in the woods and the water rushing past our feet was poetry. The idea of it made me shiver with pleasure.

Also in his strongbox is a Bible that belonged to my grandmother. It is filled with things she could not bear to throw away.

A postcard from her sister in Boston.
Inspirational poems she clipped from the newspaper.

An envelope containing four locks of my father's baby hair tied with blue ribbons and two tiny baby teeth.

I hold in my middle-aged hand all that remains of my father's body—little treasures that he has allowed my grandmother to hand to me over so many years. His curls are so fine, and golden, and the teeth gleam in the evening light, tiny milk pearls.

from

In the Lobster Capital of the World
by Don Hannah

Premiered at the Tarragon Theatre, Toronto, 1988, directed by Andy McKim. Script available from Playwrights Guild of Canada.

· · ·

"Brothers"

> *ED is talking to his brother Michael about their late father, and about keeping his sexuality a secret from his family.*

EDWARD

(pausing) I kept coming back here. Comin' back here waitin' for somebody to say something—to say, you did okay, that's alright—you made a mistake, we all make mistakes. Just one time for Dad not to act like I've got the plague. He'd give me that look, he'd just come into the room like every move I made was wrong. *(pausing)* I keep dreaming about me walking down the stairs and he's at the bottom and I think, "The wrong stairs, I came down, the wrong stairs again," cause he's gonna say, "What's in your room Ed?" like I've got a big secret that scares me shitless up there. I can be dreaming about you or David, anything, then it all changes, and I think, "oh God it's the Dad thing again." And I keep coming back here waitin' for my friggin' old man to come down outta the sky and talk to me one time. But he never did and now it's never gonna happen. *(pausing)* I keep thinking about him in the hospital after his last stroke, waking up all confused, not knowing how he got there. Sayin', "Where am I? Was I in a car accident?" And all I could think of was I'd just met David and I couldn't let any of them know. I just felt so pointless… I'm sorry, Mike, I'm sorry.

from

The Shooting Stage
by Michael Lewis MacLennan

Premiered at the Firehall Arts Centre, Vancouver, 2001, directed by
Stephane Kirkland. Script available from Playwrights Canada Press.

• • •

> MALCOLM *is a lawyer whose life is unravelling after his wife's
> death last year. At the same time, he has agreed to represent an
> art photographer Len (to whom he speaks here) who has recently
> been charged with obscenity.*

MALCOLM

I'm at this video arcade downtown, few months back. God knows why.
Couldn't handle the house. There's this kid with his back to me, scrawny,
lean strips of muscle under his thin T-shirt. He's still growing, small sleeves
tight under his armpits. He sways and jabs in front of the screen. I'm beside
him when the game finishes, give him another quarter. This time he loses
almost right away. I ask if he wants ice cream and his eyes narrow. Sure, he
says. Sure. Dairy Queen, I buy him what he wants and watch him eat it, his
skinny arms encircle the dish like a fortress. When he's done I take him to
the park. I unzip his pants and kneel before him, encircle him with my
mouth. He gasps, astonished, his soft skin has never been touched by
anyone, and for a moment I'm almost happy. His legs wobble like he's
going to faint and so I prop him against the tree, wrap my arms around
his shaking thighs and thrust him into my face. Inhale the beauty of this
unkempt perfection, the smell of youth turning.

He comes quickly. I stand up, taller than him again. He sneers at me,
probably just nervous, trying to be brave. But hey, it's this look he's giving
me, his eyes, they…. How DARE you SNEER at me, EH? EH? You little
PUNK! And I grab his flimsy arm, his mocking eyes are desperate now,
and I deliver a blow to his soft belly, send *him* bent over now. I strike that
body maybe five times, he's on the ground, and that's it, enough is enough.
Sobbing silent into the dirt. I throw him fifty dollars. The red bill lands
next to his face. His breath ruffles an edge. He's not looking at me now.

Next morning, I've forgotten. Go out there, into the day like nothing happened. Other people, they don't see what I've done. They don't know. And I start to think, "It wasn't that bad, nothing really happened... nothing really happened."

Week later, I'm back at the arcade. When he sees me, he just takes his hands from the game and turns to me, lets his rented hero explode on the screen behind him. I show him a quarter and he holds out his hand. I press the token, hard enough to leave a circle over the lines on his palm. He came back. He came back again. To me.

from

Taking Liberties
by Dave Carley

Premiered at the Alumnae Theatre, Toronto, 1992, directed by Stephen Ouimette. Script available from Playwrights Guild of Canada.

• • •

"Gerald Harvie"

GERALD Harvie is a young father, about 30. He has recently set up an accounting practice in Ashburnham, a small Ontario city. The era is the 1950s and a good job, with a wife and child on the way, in a postcard perfect town—it should be a wonderful life. It's not. Gerald Harvie is homosexual. And some nights, when he works late, the temptation to step outside the boundaries of "acceptable behaviour" grows too much.

At the start of this monologue, Gerald has been walking through the downtown. It's late. He is trying to turn homeward.

GERALD

The sidewalks pull me alone. Pull me east. Pull me east, away from Claire, pull me to the park. To the park, dark breath of green; exhaling slow and clear and dark, sound receding, sounds of city sliding off behind the trees. Twisted path. Curve. Curve and dip. Duck for branch. I walk in darkness. Down through the ravine. Up through the ravine. Knowing each dipping branch, each blocking log, knowing, knowing all these things and letting myself be pulled along.

Branch brushes face. Scratch. Blood? How do I explain blood? Blood on my handkerchief. Then: ground hard as I cross the green, soft again as I slip into the trees.

Dirt breathing out. Exhaling. Carcass of rotting animal. Thread of smoke. Tobacco smoke.

Snap of twig. Fallen leaves. Leaf rustle. Rustle. Squirrel? Rat?

Glow of cigarette. Then dark. Then glow. A shape. I come close. No. No. No. I back away.

Freedom: to belong, to exist.

Strength: to be a husband, a father. To leave here. To turn away, turn home, walk home to my Claire, walk west to my Claire, to shut her reddened eyes with kisses, to walk home to her. Yes. Yes. I can do it.

No.

I turn downtown again.

There is another place. There is something I need and something I want and I know where it is.

Smell of bus, lingering smells of bus and crowds; people leaving town, good people leaving town, good people returning, destinations announced, good people greeted, people ignored, names called out, people walking through crowds unnoticed and now me, my steps ringing across deserted pavement, almost no one here now. Almost no one here.

I'm inside. There's a door. I open it and I walk down the stairs. I walk down the stairs until I reach the bottom and now there are two more doors. I am drawn to one and I go inside.

God forgive me.

I am here now. Are you there?

I have crept into the bowels of the city. I have crept here and now I stand and pretend and hope. I catch his gaze, then I look away. I look back, look away, look back and now I am no longer even in my body. I have fled that prison and I am flying a thousand, a hundred thousand miles above this green and pleasant town. I am looking back at myself walking over to my fellow human and I'm only feeling this incredible freedom and this great overwhelming rush of liberty and, finally, finally: power.

from

The Shooting Stage
by Michael Lewis MacLennan

Premiered at the Firehall Arts Centre, Vancouver, 2001, directed by Stephane Kirkland. Script available from Playwrights Canada Press.

• • •

LEN defends himself and his art against an obscenity charge.

LEN

You might call it obscene; I always saw it as art.

Because you have to use your imagination to see the whole picture.

Describe a photograph. Your Honour, isn't that redundant?

Ah. The "record." Very well. For the "record," a teenage boy is wearing a... crimson dress. *(He looks up, cued to continue.)* His body is... well, he's sexually aroused. The face is... obscured. I believe he was sixteen.

I didn't "make" him do anything.

Mister Prosecutor, you may have been an exception, but I doubt there's a sixteen-year-old boy alive who needs any cajoling to jerk off.

Apologies for making the Crown blush.

No, I don't believe I did anything wrong.

I know about the laws. I know he's only sixteen. But you see, *sir*, I myself was fourteen years old when I took that photograph. Rather changes things, doesn't it?

You see, a photograph's not a bullet. It can't be so clearly traced to its origins.

I have no idea where he is. It was more than twenty years ago.

(looking at the photograph) I included it in the exhibition because I found it beautiful.

Here, in the urgent thrust of the forearm. The way his neck is tight from his frantic labour. How vulnerable his body seems, the thin dress strap on the verge of falling. Beautiful. Dresses like this, it's like they're made for adolescent boys.

Actually, I'd forgotten all about it. Came across it, few months before the show.

We all have these photos, slipped in the pages of a diary, the bottom of a shoe box. The kind you never look at but can't bear to throw out. They were taken to arrest time, snapped just before something in the picture leaves. A person, a feeling…. Taken because we find time is galloping too quickly. You'll lose these photos as you do anything you put away too carefully.

from

The Bends
by James O'Reilly

Premiered at the Tarragon Theatre, Toronto, 1989, directed by Julian Richings. Script available from Playwrights Canada Press.

• • •

Under the following text Johnny meanders about the outdoor playing space in a rough mime version of DAVID's narrative.

DAVID

Johnny McLeod walks down an alleyway behind the IGA, throwing stones against the wall and buzzing his lips to mimic the sound of urine passing through a fan. He spots some garbage against the brick wall below a loading dock and zeros in on a green cigarette package—his mother's brand. The smell of menthol smoke in his memory makes him stop for a moment and walk over to the rustling garbage. He picks up the faded green box and thinks about last New Year's when his mother made him go to the store and buy two packs so she could sit up all night with his grandmother. The night her boyfriend didn't show up. His mother and grandmother just sat up all night drinking, crying, talking, and smoking cigarettes. Most of the time though they just sat, saying nothing, with the lights off, curling the ashes from their cigarettes against the lip of a huge, green, porcelain ashtray shaped like a bird. Johnny used to call it "the duck ashtray." He remembers playing "duckpond" on the living room table, the one his mother used to rest her feet on when she watched TV. The wood-grain looked like cat's eyes and the sea to him. The current runs swiftly through his mind now as he clutches the empty green cigarette package. From beyond the periphery of his attention, his left hand opens to release three warm stones to the ground. As they hit, the child envisions green ripples, concentric circles, forming on the surface of a wood-grained sea mapped out over the seamless expanse of a menthol cigarette package.

from

Possible Worlds
by John Mighton

Premiered at the Canadian Stage Company at the St. Lawrence Centre, Toronto, 1990, directed by Peter Hinton. Script available from Playwrights Canada Press.

• • •

GEORGE

I remember once… I found myself walking down a residential street late at night. There were no trees and a huge moon in the sky. All the houses were made of wood with small windows and phosphorescent geometric flowers painted on the shutters. I was lost. I went up to one of the houses and knocked. A tall, grey being, shaped like a human but with no nose answered. He wore a short tunic with jewelled medallions and said, "Come in will ya?" I noticed there was no furniture. The family was all seated on the floor. I stepped in and they clapped—they had hands—and the tall, grey being rippled as he walked as if he had no bones. The woman of the house looked like a chicken. When I got within three feet of her she turned around and expanded her backside like a huge rose—she was giving off some sort of scent to welcome me. Standing in the shadows I saw a man I thought I knew. He took my arm and led me out to a field where two men were building with a pile of small rocks.

from

Blue Blazes
by Torquil Colbo

Premiered at the Resource Centre for the Arts, St. John's, 1998, directed by Andy Jones. Script available from the playwright at forkwill@yahoo.com.

• • •

"Balthazar"

Balthazar FISK believes that he is in constant danger of spontaneously combusting—of bursting into flames. He feels that the only way to avoid horrible death is to become extremely angry at the first thing that presents itself. The rage burns off or diverts the energy that otherwise would consume him. Thus, in this monologue, when he is seized by the fit, he can only complete it by getting very, very angry at the subject of his tale. As you might imagine, this condition has made it difficult for him to function in society. When we first meet him here he has voluntarily committed himself to a mental institution. If you like, he could be testing himself, addressing a mirror or an imaginary audience. He needs to see if he can function, and decides to test a speech. What begins as tentative would gain in enthusiasm as he finds that he is able, after all this time, to speak out loud at length. The attack would be tremendously disappointing to him, but he doggedly tries to complete the tale.

FISK is standing in a pool of light. He is wearing institutional pyjamas and a dressing gown.

FISK

There's a story, an old story, I'm trying to remember. I think I heard it in… childhood? Yeah and it's a fable. There are these two guys, they're at a train station and they're waiting for the train. Oh, and one of them's a normal guy like you or… well, like you. The other one's a uh… he's a Martian. And the train station's on the moon, it's one of the stops for the Interplanetary express. But it's been delayed. Solar flares or some such space hazard.

So the man and the Martian, they're two guys who wouldn't normally sit and talk, but there's only one empty table left in the spaceport cafeteria. They have to share. And what do you know? they find out that they have a lot in common. They're both going to Jupiter on business. They're both avid birdwatchers, and they trade some Martian and Earthling birdcalls. Like ah… *(makes a weird howling warble)* That was a Martian bird.

They've both been to Venus. Stayed at the same hotel as a matter of fact. They celebrate their new friendship by ordering a couple of bubbling black Venusian coffees. They toast each other's health, they toast their favourite zero gravity polo teams, they toast the women in their lives. Both are proud family men. They show each other family photos; the Earthling's son, daughter and dog, the Martian's giant egg sac. Everything's hunky dory.

Then. The Earthling does something that the Martian finds a little strange. The Earthling takes his bubbling black Venusian coffee and he BLOWS ON IT.

"What are you doing there, pal?" asks the Man from Mars. He's a little puzzled.

"Why," says the Earthling, "The coffee's a little hot for me. I can't drink it like this."

"So you blow on it?"

"Well yeah, it cools the coffee."

"Huh. Fascinating. You learn something new every day."

The Martian actually finds this a little weird, but he lets it go. Soon the two of them have finished their coffees, the train's about to arrive, they're standing out on the tarmac… *(BALTHAZAR suddenly clutches his stomach and stops, just as his story is getting into its rhythm. He clutches his stomach and starts to choke.)* …They're standing on the…. AAAh! *(He bangs on his stomach.)* Fuck! Fuck! Fuck! Get out of here, stupid fuck! I'm in the middle of a story! Aaaarggh!

> *He falls on the floor thrashing about for a bit, yelling nonsensically. Eventually he recovers, stands and tries to resume his story. Until the end of this monologue he's shivering and trying to fight off the attack.*

So they're out on the landing pad having a grand old chat. And one thing about the surface of the moon, it's cold there, very cold. So they're shivering a bit. And the earthling takes his hands and he cups them like this, and then what does he do? He blows into them.

"What are you doing?" asks the Martian. "Aren't your hands cold enough already?"

"What? Oh no," and the Earthling laughs. "This time I'm blowing on my hands to warm them."

And the Man from Mars turns a paler shade of green. And he backs away, his arms are raised to ward off the earthling. He's calling on all his Martian saints to preserve him.

"What? What's the problem?"

"Get back, Demon! Go to Hell!"

"Oh come on, pal. It's me, Larry…"

"I don't know you! Take the next train, Hellspawn. I will not travel with any man who can summon both hot and cold with one breath!"

Which just goes to show…. Aaaarghhh! Nyyaaa! No, not yet! I haven't got to the moral yet! AAAAA! STUPID SHIT FUCK MARTIAN DICKWADS! LITTLE GREEN SNOT-FOR-BRAINS BIGOT! I'LL BASH YOUR POINTY LITTLE MARTIAN HEAD IN! KILL! KILL! KILL! AAAaaaaarggghhhh… aaaaah.

FISK's hands clench at his sides and he starts quivering, standing bolt upright, as tense as possible. A kind of whimper escapes him now and then, like steam from a kettle.

from

I, Claudia
by Kristen Thomson

Premiered at the Tarragon Theatre, Toronto, 2001, directed by Chris Abraham. Script available from Playwrights Canada Press.

• • •

> *DRACHMAN, a theatre artist in his home country of Bulgonia, works as a janitor in Canada. He tells a fable about experience and wisdom.*

DRACHMAN

To conclude, I would like to tell you famous Bulgonian fable, very short story, that my mother was telling to me when I was crying and so I was telling to my son, and so of course this story I am loving very much. Yeah, I have a son, twenty-two, he is live in United State—but we are not talking on that.

Once upon a time, in a land as close as your thoughts, a naughty little Spragnome was climbing through the window of a tiny straw hut and peek into the cradle of a newborn baby and whisper to her sleeping parents this promise. "Weave this child a basket to contain all what her heart desires and when it is full, I will return to make her wise." Now, I must stop to tell you that in Bulgonia we know this Spragnome very well. He is very tiny, like my thumb, particular type of gnome which seem to do one thing, but always he is doing something else. So, to continue. Next morning, the farmer is cutting the straw and his wife is weaving that basket and for many years that child she take her basket and she go in her life gathering, gathering, gathering everything that her little heart want. Until her basket is so full. And when it's so full she have to put it down. Now, it's too heavy. Even so much pleasure, ya, it's not possible to carry on like that endlessly. You know. So she put her basket and so she go and she have a little sleep, something, and when she wake up she come back to find that her basket is completely empty! How did this happen? Well, on this moment, after such a long years, that naughty little Spragnome is appear to her. She point on that crazy midget yelling "Thief!" And she begin to search on him and searching on every place for her stolen possessions until she see that she cannot find one thing, not one hope remaining. All is gone. And so, she collapse on her basket and begin weeping, "Now I have nothing left but my sadness." And so she cry and she keep to cry until practical flood of tears was filling her basket. And when her basket is complete full of tears that Spragnome point. He say: "Now, you see, your basket is no longer empty. Now it have very much inside. *Lugaldya.* Look." And when she look she saw that her basket was become a deep pool... brimming with her experience and dancing on the surface of her tears... yes, very clearly she perceived it. Reflected on the surface of her grief she saw herself.

from

Here Lies Henry
by Daniel MacIvor and Daniel Brooks

Premiered at the Six Stages Festival at Buddies in Bad Times Theatre, Toronto, 1995, directed and dramaturged by Daniel Brooks. Script available from Playwrights Canada Press.

• • •

HENRY gets closer to telling the truth.

HENRY

I know you.

You have dreams. Dreams about dreams about flying, dreams about falling, dreams that you don't understand. You have landscapes in your mind that you call your own. You try to be humble. You try to be honest. You know that it's better to keep your mouth shut and your eyes open, but it's very hard to do. You look for some small way to have some small way to have some small measure of immortality, but you're concerned that there will be nobody left to care. You hope that one day you will understand something, but worry that maybe that's not the point. You wonder what's the big deal about sex anyway, and then suddenly, brilliantly remember. You go to the movies, you think some of them are good and some of them are bad. You go to plays, even though you hate to be bored. Some nights you look up into the sky and remember what it was like before everything felt so poisoned. And you think that love is a good thing.

See. I know you.

from

Patience
by Jason Sherman

Premiered at the Tarragon Theatre, Toronto, 1998, directed by Ian Prinsloo.
Script available from Playwrights Canada Press.

• • •

"A Tragic Story"

*On the way to visit their dying brother, PHIL tells Reuben about
a life-changing encounter.*

PHIL

You might as well be the first to know. I'm leaving Mary. I know. I met
somebody. A student. Christ. Every year, I worry about this. Every year, the
students get more gorgeous. Or maybe I just get less picky. But you know
me, I always kept my distance. I was always so careful. Especially with the
crap going on now on campus, where all you need to do is look at a student
and—shit, would you look at this again? You got that map? Try to find the
next exit. Anyway, the thing is, this year, there's this girl in my class, and she
is, she is very special. I mean, brilliant. Not even beautiful, in any conven-
tional sense, you know? Just out of the ordinary, from the inside. She has
such intelligence, and she's so alive. She was trained as a pianist, a classical
pianist, then, it's a tragic story, her father died, and shortly after she was
diagnosed with this nervous disorder, where, if she played for any length of
time, her hands would begin to shake, uncontrollably shake, which, as you
can imagine, for a concert pianist, is something of a liability. So that was
the end of it. Of the piano playing. But, the vivacity of this girl, she couldn't
be held back; she could do anything she wants, but what does she choose?
Wants to become a physicist. I think it's because—I think it makes sense,
because of the mathematics involved. You know? The mathematics of
music and of physics, there's a natural—anyway, we would talk about this,
at length, you see, and that was the problem. Because as we're talking,
and—alright, dammit, I agreed to go out for a drink with her, on campus,
one night, told Mary I had a faculty meeting, shit, I hated to lie, because
I knew it would be the beginning to more and more lies but, there it is, I'm
only a man, I'm only human, I made a mistake and it grew. One night, she

began to speak about celestial music, my God, I fell in love with her that very moment. Here we go, it's picking up again. No, I *already* was in love with her, what I did was I gave in to it. Then I did something I've never done in my life: we went to a motel, it was her idea, Rube, a cheap fifties motel on the lakeshore strip, and the bed squeaked and the curtains were torn and it smelled like goddamn stale cigarettes but we tore off each other's clothes and fucked like dogs for hours, it was bliss, every position known to man, we even invented a few, it was otherwordly, I mean that, I was transported, I was in another fucking time zone, Rube, and we lay there, covered in cum and sweat, and we laughed, we laughed and laughed and, Jesus, in the space of a single night, I experienced more with this girl than I did with Mary in twenty years of marriage. Rube, Rube, I know we've talked about this, I know that because of what happened with Mom and Dad we swore to each other we'd never repeat their mistakes, but dammit Rube for the first time in my life I'm in ecstasy, I've met the woman I was meant to be with. I have to be with her. I'm going to be with her.

> *Beat.*

She's nineteen. Don't for God's sake judge me. I'm drawn to this girl, Rube, I can't help myself. If I don't go with her, I'll never be happy. I'll never know. Do you know what I'm talking about? Has anything like this ever happened to you? In all honesty now. Have you ever met a woman you knew you had to be with, and you denied it: you said, "I will wait," because of circumstance, because of conscience, because of everything but instinct, said, "I will wait until the day comes when I can be with her." And then it's too late. You know, this whole thing with Johnny…. You have to act now, you have to move on your passions or you'll wither and die. You'll be walking around dead, and that's that. Has that ever happened to you? Has it?

from

Atlantis
by Maureen Hunter

Premiered at the Manitoba Theatre Centre, Winnipeg, co-produced by
Theatre Calgary, 1996. Script available from Scirocco Drama.

• • •

> Atlantis *is set on the Greek island of Santorini in 1985. BEN is*
> *a Canadian living there in self-imposed exile. In this monologue,*
> *he has just fallen in love with Mircea, a woman of the island.*

BEN

I came up the hill this afternoon like a man who had suddenly sprouted
wings. I mean it when I say this: I didn't walk, I flew.

And all the way up my heart was in turmoil. Would she be waiting for me
in her doorway? Would she reach out to me as she has before? But again
I had nothing to give her, no carving, no excuse to touch her, to let my
fingers graze her fingers, there, in the bright light of day, in full view in
the street. What an act of anarchy that's been, I see this now. What erotic
license we have taken with each other: to stand there, in broad daylight,
and let our fingers touch.

She wasn't standing in her doorway, she was standing in the street. In
a dress the colour of the sea. Her hair tied simply at the neck, tied loosely
like an open invitation. With one finger, in my mind as I approached,
I pulled the ribbon from her hair and set it free. Wove my fingers through
it, lifted it and let it fall, buried my face in it, breathed deeply, breathed it in
as though it held the breath of life.

All this in my mind, or so I thought.

Until I felt her arms go round me, felt her body shudder, and realized the
thing I'd just imagined.

I'd just done.

from

Adult Entertainment
by George F. Walker

Premiered at the Factory Theatre, Toronto, 1997, directed by George F. Walker. Script available from Talonbooks.

• • •

MAX

Five years ago. A domestic... Donny and I just stumbled on it. Came around a corner and there was this guy, about sixty-five, beating the crap out of his wife with a baseball bat. Right in the middle of the street... I'm thinking what is this fucking ugly garbage. Who needs this. But we couldn't just ignore it. So we hop outta the car, Donny goes to the old woman who's a bloody pulp by now, and I get the husband's attention to... distract him... yell at him or something.... Yeah I think I yelled "Hey you fat prick." Anyway he turns. Starts coming at me with the bat.... He's this big mean ugly old drunk, and he's got his wife's blood all over his face and his undershirt and he's coming at me mumbling some insane nonsense. And I'm backing up.... He's getting closer.... And then I hear Donny yelling. "Drop him. Drop him, Maxie! Shoot him or he's gonna crush your brains with that thing." So I do... I shoot him. Once. Right through the heart.... And he drops like the sack of shit he is. And then... it was all over except for the paperwork.... That night I got drunker than I'd ever been before... or since really.... And I'm thinking "When I get up tomorrow morning my life will be changed... I'm gonna have trouble living like this." ...But when I get up... that's not how I feel. I look around at my kids and what I feel is... I was doing my job.... And anybody who ever comes at me and threatens my life, carrying a bat, a knife, a gun, a saw, a fucking stick... is gonna die.... That's just what has to happen... *(shrugs)*

from

The House of Sonya
by Floyd Favel

Premiered at The Club, Regina, produced by Takwakin Performance Lab, 2000, directed by Floyd Favel. Script available from the playwright, Box 272, Paynton, SK, S0M 2J0.

• • •

"Astrov Visiting Kokum Marina"

Dr. ASTROV has dropped by Uncle Vanya's house to check up on the professor, where the professor, his new wife Elena and Sonya are visiting. ASTROV is attracted to Elena, the professor's wife. ASTROV is in the kitchen talking with Kokum Marina, the maid.

ASTROV

I've become a different man. I've worked myself to the bone trying to make something of myself. I haven't had a day of rest in months. When I lie in bed at night I hope that I don't get dragged off to see another patient. Do you think I get thanks for this?

Still they say, a *moniakasoot*! he acts like a white man! for what? because I care?

It's a dull pointless dreary life, and it gets me down. Around me, all I hear is who's seeing who, who's stealing money. Aren't there other things to talk about?

I haven't lost my intelligence, thank God, but somehow my feelings are blunted.

A few weeks ago Indian Affairs sent me up north. Modernization had laid waste to all that God had given. Time is supposed to help these people, instead, 20 to 40 percent of the adult population has diabetes and heart problems. They have nothing to do. To be in their villages is to be in a village of invalids surrounded by a forest whose soul is being ripped out and which the spirits have abandoned. What can live in a land laid waste by machines and money!

I was on my feet all day and when I got home, there was still no rest. They brought in this young woman beaten by her husband. I administered to her needs and when it was the last thing I needed, my feelings came to life. I raged at how badly we treat one another. I sat down and I shut my eyes and I thought, will the people who come after us in a hundred years, will they treat each other better? will our land be healed? will they remember who they are and who we were?

from

Consecrated Ground
by George Boyd

Premiered at the Sir James Dunn Theatre, Halifax, produced by Eastern
Front Theatre, 1999, directed by Richard Donat. Script available from
Talonbooks.

• • •

> *A Brief Synopsis by George Boyd.*
> Consecrated Ground *is set in the mid-sixties in Africville, Nova
> Scotia—a small suburb of Halifax.*
> *Africville, one of the oldest, black indigenous communities was
> set to be bulldozed by the tractors of city hall, meanwhile the
> community is in an uproar.*
> *Because the community was nestled next to the city dump
> and habourside, wharf rats were prevalent. One has in fact,
> consumed the baby Tully—Willem's and Clarice's child. Willem,
> not a native of Africville, is set to pull stakes because of the
> appalling living conditions. Clarice, however, is adamant that
> they stay.*
> *The following scene consists of WILLEM's argument for the
> move.*

WILLEM

(whispering) Leasey? *(She doesn't answer.)* Leasey? *(pause)* I just stand here
and look up through the window into the stars, ya know, Leasey? *(pause)*
I kin see... I kin see before all those twinkling stars that the Big Dipper and
Venus be as bright... as bright as the Star of David, baby... *(pause)* Leasey,
I—

> *CLARICE shifts, her eyes open wide.*

It like... it like the whole universe out there, just waitin' for us to... step
out into it.... Like, baby, I been thinkin'... maybe it's time we got outta
Africville... and... and, well, there ain't hardly no one left here anyways.
Everybody's gonna go. I'm thinkin' yeah... maybe we should take the city's
offer and sell. People always movin', Leasey. White folks move all the time.

Mister Clancy say we can relocate to a good, warm place in, ah, Uniacke Square.

CLARICE doesn't stir, but stays perfectly still.

I'm thinkin'… maybe now's the time to leave. See, the city ain't too happy with all the publicity it's gittin' in the papers and stuff and so… well, they wanna make a deal with us. They got big plans for this land. They talkin' like a park and maybe some industry and stuff. *(pause)* yeah… Mister Clancy mentioned a park or sumpin'… Leasey, I dunno… don'tcha see what this means for us? Now's our chance to get out—get a good price for our land, 'cause the city wants it bad and it don't want no trouble. Know what I mean?

CLARICE doesn't answer.

There ain't nothin' we kin do, Leasey. Can't you see that? If the city wants our land, they're gonna take it and it don't matter what the nigger wants. Never has, never will… Leasey you listenin' to me? Are you listenin', baby?

CLARICE suddenly turns to him, sound asleep.

from

Easy Lenny Lazmon and the Great Western Ascension
by Anton Piatigorsky

Premiered at the Annex Theatre, Toronto, produced by Moriah Productions and Go Chicken Go, 1998, directed by Chris Abraham. Script available from Playwrights Canada Press.

• • •

> *MAYER is a small-town, desert, cattle rancher. He is trying to convince Easy, an ambitious young man, to come live on his real, quotidian ranch instead of pursuing the more mystical and dangerous ranch of Easy's dreams.*

MAYER

One of the first settlers of our town. A famous pioneer. When I met him, he was an ancient man, walked with a cane. Mayor of this town once, long before me. Served on the city council, and school board. Old Black Jack and Sophia were close friends for some years. Hours a day, they'd sit out on our front porch, watching the horizon, whispering. Sure. One time I heard a story about his past. When Black Jack Yvenson was a young man, he headed west with three of his bravest and strongest companions. West, he said, to a great ranch on the coast. These four men were well-educated, sharp, strong. The best of the best of the west. They made it to that ranch, past all the challenges of the road. Four men entered. But only one man left intact. Just Black Jack. He came out alone. His hair now white as the salt flats, his eyes filled with the flame of the land. So the story goes.

What happened to the other three? "The best of the best," Black Jack said, "but still not good enough." The first, apparently, did himself in with one shot from his Colt. Too much for him to bear. The second was tortured until he went insane. For years after, he wandered from town to town, drunk, no shoes on his feet. And the third… the other, a famous outlaw… why, they cut him down, right at his shoots. But Black Jack was left alone. Only he was strong enough to survive the ranch. And there he lived for many years. Until he decided to leave.

You hear me, son? He left. Sure! Abandoned that glorious ranch and came back to this arid, little stop. Why? Well Black Jack once said to me: "An endless ranch is like an endless road. You pass over each hill blind and alone."

The endless word. The endless ranch. That could never be your home, Easy, no. It's nobody's home. Old Black Jack knew better. And Sophia, despite what she may say, she knows better, too. Black Jack came back here, instead, helped set up a desert town for young travellers. For folks needing nothing more than a break from the road. A solid home, a place to settle down after a long and failing journey. Sure. For people like me and Sophia. And for you, Easy. It's not perfect land, you see. Black Jack knew that. But it's possible to live here and to breathe.

from

Horse High, Bull Strong, Pig Tight
by Kent Stetson

Premiered at The Arts Guild, Charlottetown, produced by Theatre PEI, 2001, directed by Kent Stetson. Script available from Playwrights Canada Press.

• • •

> PETER Stewart, in his late seventies and afflicted with terminal cancer, walks to the top field of his 150-acre PEI farm, clad only in pyjamas on the coldest January night in living memory. He has decided to join his wife whose death he has not completely mourned. PETER's plan to slip quiet into the cold beneath the full moon and icy stars induces a flood of memories, some borne by the woodland creatures he has always admired and loved, and some by the souls of the departed who shaped and filled his life. In the following excerpt, PETER recalls his first visit to "a perfect farm."

PETER

I never seen it fail.
A good farmer makes a dandy boss.
I worked for farmers whose lands was always in top form.
Every body for miles cryin' drought or flood
Blight or bugs or this or that.
You'd walk onto a good farm in bad times
And honest to God...
The feelin' of the place.
I'd say heaven on earth.

The first thing you notice is the fences.
Barbed wire singin' tight,
Stapled to good solid fir posts, striped and painted.
Limed, in the old days.

Either side of the lane,
If the house and barns are set back a ways,

There'll be a pair of fields the sight of which
Will do your heart good.

Over there's a stand of timothy,
A day or two before comin' into head.
Today's the day he'll cut her.
He'll have her down and tedded,
Raked, coiled, pitched and stowed within two days.

And there's twelve acres of seed Sebagos,
Just comin' into bloom.
Not a hint of mosaic, black leg, leaf roll—
Rogued to perfection.
Not a lamb's quarter
Nor a show of mustard to be seen.
No sir.

Behind the house is a stand of clover.
The smell waftin' in the bedroom window
First thing on a July mornin',
Man dear.
You wake up whistlin'!

The pond by the road
Is quackin' full of big fat Muscovy ducks.
White geese are flappin' and honkin'
And goin' on somethin' wicket.

The pasture's some lush, eh?
The cows goin' at it like there's no tomorrow...
Bags full to burstin',
Teats stickin' straight out sideways,
Waitin' for ya at the gate to the barn,
Bawlin' for relief,
They're that full of milk.

Calves buntin' and suckin'
Jumpin' and runnin',
'Till of a sudden
Their hind quarters hunkers down,
Their front legs fold's under...

Out on the pasture,
There's not a calf awake or standin'.

The cows soon follow.
Down they go.
Up come their cuds.

And down comes the rain.

The soil sucks up moisture like a sponge.
You can hear it seepin' in.

It pours, boys.
Grass, leaves, fruits and berries drip water.
Everything's washed clean.
Just... shinin' clean.

from

Drumheller or Dangerous Times
by Gordon Pengilly

Premiered at the Prime Stock Theatre Company, Red Deer, 2001,
directed by Thomas Usher. Script available from the playwright at
gpeng@spots.ca.

• • •

> *John GALLAGHER, 40, a coal miner with a hard jaw and*
> *a harder disposition, stands on a rocky ledge overlooking the*
> *badlands in the setting sun. A night owl screeches. There's the*
> *loud rap of a mallet and GALLAGHER steps forward into*
> *a different light, a courtroom from five years earlier.*

GALLAGHER

I didn't kill John Coward, Your Worship, and I don't know who did.
I counted John as a friend. I was in the Great War and learned the value
of friendship the hard way. The young man closest to me over there died
in my arms and he'd saved my life only hours before. I wept Goddamnit.
I bawled like a baby. I'd never been afraid of anything on earth before that
tour of duty and now I'm afraid of thunder and lightning which I used to
love.

Anyway, the very next day, I get popped in the head by a sniper's bullet.
Goes right through my helmet. Next thing I know I'm on horseback riding
through sagebrush on the side of a hill overlooking the Red Deer River.
I'm wearing a uniform I don't recognize and all I know is that my horse is
named Spirit. I think I've died and crossed over, of course. Then I hear the
cry of a coyote nearby and I follow it to a patch of crocus where I find the
poor beast caught in a trap. Its leg is terribly mangled. It's mad with pain
and lunges and snaps at me.

Well, there's nothing left to do—I take out my service revolver and I shoot
it. And just then everything goes black and when I open my eyes again I'm
lying in a hospital bed in London, England. My whole head is bandaged up
like an Indian turban. The nurse tells me I've been in a coma for three and

a half weeks. I don't remember my dream about the coyote but I distinctly smell crocus.

Now if that isn't strange enough, Your Worship, when I come home from that fucking bloodbath I join up with the newly-formed Alberta Provincial Police. You can see what's coming. One day I'm riding my horse named Spirit on the side of a hill overlooking the Red Deer River and I hear a coyote crying which is caught in a trap. I have the strongest sense that I've been here before and when I shoot the beast I flash back to the battlefield and I live through my good friend's death again.

Now the story's been offered here as evidence against me that every so often without warning I lapse into a kind of spell which can last for several minutes and when I come out of it I often have some memory loss. It's because of that wound to my head in the war. But what I've not told anybody until this very moment is when that spell happens I have hallucinations sometimes of the things to come. I once had a vision of myself sitting right here in this dock, Your Worship, and I'm sure you think that's funny but I know you're going to sentence me to swing today.

Now you're probably wondering what I'm getting at. Well I'm getting at this, that though I may be damaged goods in some respects and though I may be rough at times and though I may have killed in the war—I'm not a murderer. I feel like a coyote caught in a trap. So if you're so certain I killed John Coward then I beg you to take me out behind the courthouse and do away with me promptly for I can think of nothing worse than sitting on death row with only my innocence for company. That would be worse than the war to me. And that's all I have to say. Thanks for your indulgence.

from

Whylah Falls: The Play
by George Elliott Clarke

Premiered at the Sir James Dunn Theatre, Halifax, produced by Eastern Front Theatre, 1997, directed by Paula Danckert. Script available from Playwrights Canada Press.

• • •

"The Testimony of Othello Clemence"

At this moment in Whylah Falls: The Play *(literally, II.6), OTHELLO Clemence speaks from beyond the grave to reveal the manner of his murder by S. Scratch Seville. The pathos of the scene, plus the resultant emotions to grief and rage for OTHELLO's surviving family and friends, serves to reunite two estranged, potential lovers, X, and OTHELLO's sister, Shelley. Although OTHELLO's killing is unjust, based on racial and sexual jealousy, it becomes the means by which X returns to* Whylah Falls. *He attends OTHELLO's funeral, and, thanks to the maturity that his encounter with death provokes, he will likely soon attend a wedding—his own. In Shakespearean terms, this scene is the mechanism by which* Othello *morphs into* Love's Labours Lost.

OTHELLO

When I felt the scream as the shot smoked… and saw the hot, red pain as it tore my stomach, splashing me back through the soft door that crumbled like thin ice, icy splinters gouging my back, and I flailed under air, I swore Scratch had drowned me. I was at peace. But that peace was pissed by terror as I crawled down his thrashing driveway, wanting water. Water. I was leaking from the hole in my stomach, my face busted, and the sight in my eyes crazy, blue, red, yellow, I wasn't much able to move, then I blurred Scratch limping slow after me, cursing his fucking door, and looming over me (I ain't lyin') with his butterknife (I know, pretty funny, 'cept it wasn't very funny for me), and drove the cold blade into my gut so hard he bent the tip.

All I could think about was having surgery. But what happened was horror. Scratch didn't once stop his attack on me. Quite the contrary. The simple bastard broke my stomach at very close range. When he feared the shot had failed, he must have gone to his kitchen, gone straight to the knife drawer, and got a butterknife, knowing it would follow the shot to my gut and leave no trace. Does that sound as though he killed in self-defence?

Make no mistake! Scratch used that knife to stab me. And when I whimpered, he stabbed me again. And when blood, instead of words, spilled from my mouth, he stabbed me again and again, and he would have gone on stabbing me til I was dead, 'cept he was scared someone would come. But it didn't matter cos I died anyway.

from

The Waterhead
by Aaron Bushkowsky

Premiered at the Playwrights Theatre Centre, Vancouver, produced by the Solo Collective Theatre, 2000, directed by Del Surjik. Script available from Playwrights Canada Press.

•••

> THE MAN visits his mother in the hospital only to find out that his father refuses to pay his respects, choosing instead to stay at the lake to fish. The mother insists that the son not go to the lake to get the father and THE MAN is deeply suspicious.

THE MAN

I find myself in a hospital. A long white corridor.

People in the halls look like they have just stumbled out of coffins, shuffling along the handrails, heads down, their skin as thin as rice-paper, a welcoming party of the dying and nearly dead. I feel like taking everybody out for a Big Mac. Get some colour in their cheeks. One of them touches my sleeve: "Help me, please, please help me…"

I compose myself near a nursing station, drinking loudly from a shiny water fountain. The hospital blares at me with its whiteness, its sick pine-tree smell tainted with more than a touch of urine, its updated Musak, Bob James doing a Beatles medley—yeah-yeah-yeah—its web of hallways and rooms, sickness and death and dying hiding behind grey curtains, and nobody seems to mind. What's wrong with these people?

When we get to her room, my mother's appearance snaps me out of it. Tubes! Tubes linking her to a bank of blinking machines, liquids steadily dripping from two bags hanging like old woman's teats above her head, her urine—liquid gold, she says—being siphoned off to another bag beside her bed.

She sees me and my lovely wife beside me and smiles. The transplant is working. The new kidney—a donation from a motorcyclist, a dead motorcyclist, she speculates—is slowly drawing the ocean from inside her to the see-through containers that surround her bed. She is making tributaries, tiny bays of herself, run-offs of DNA, blood, puke and sweat and who-knows-what and she knows I can't stand to see her like this, calmly draining her insides for everybody to see and I want to tell my wife I can't take it anymore, I want to tell her I'm scared and embarrassed and sick of thinking we're all going to die some day and I just want to go home and eat popcorn, watch "Baywatch" and forget about everything. Just forget I was ever born because some day, I know this will be me on a different machine. Same kidneys I'm afraid.

Then my mother sees me frowning and fidgeting and looking around at the get-well cards, the semi-dry flowers guarding the window near the fire extinguisher, the tiny dead TV hanging like a snake from the ceiling, and she licks her dry lips and points at me with a shaking, grey finger.

"I'm going to live," she says weakly. "It's a nice feeling. I just hope this doesn't happen to you."

And then she falls asleep.

from

The Stone Angel
by James W. Nichol
based on the novel by Margaret Laurence

Premiered at the Blyth Festival, 1991, directed by Brian Richmond. Script available from Playwrights Canada Press.

• • •

"Lees' Cross"

In adapting Margaret Laurence's novel to the stage, and with the play originally running much too long, this long monologue from a minor character (I know, there's no such thing) was an obvious candidate to get cut. However, my instinct told me it was too important a speech because it spoke to the theme of the novel. And to my surprise and delight, this particular speech has always played as one of the strongest moments in the play.

LEES, a salesman and alcoholic, has stumbled on ninety-year-old Hagar, who has run away from an old age home, while LEES is hiding in his favourite drinking spot, an old fish cannery by the sea. He offers her a drink and tells her his story.

LEES

I had a son... but I lost him. Oh, it was a while ago now... a few years ago.

LOTTIE picks up the tea service and exits.

(offering HAGAR the bottle) Want some more?

HAGAR takes the bottle, drinks from it.

Yeah... five years ago, to be exact. Last March. Lou... that's my wife... she'd just as soon I not talk about it. Lou and me... we met at church. Bible camp. In those days, she could pray for hours, fervent as an angel... and when she lay down on the moss and spread those great white thighs of hers... there wasn't a sweeter place in this entire world!

Of course, we had to get married sooner than we'd planned. Didn't bother me, but it sure bothered Lou. All of a sudden she became a worrier...

planned to tell everybody the baby was premature. She hardly ate a thing except tomatoes... very low calorie, you know... but nevertheless, when Donnie was born he weighed nine pounds, twelve ounces. What a disaster!

She thought it was a punishment from God. Some punishment... a whopping big healthy beautiful baby boy! But she never saw it that way at all. She changed. Her heart didn't seem to be so much in life anymore. But she was twice as keen on Tabernacle. She still is. Not me.

At first I went along with it. She got all involved with this preacher called Pulsifer. He was prophesying the end of time and we were going to Tabernacle every night to pray for the exact date. I guess I got tired of the wait. One night the floor I was kneeling on felt like iron and all I could think of was that the crease in my pants was ruined. I looked around... and old Pulsifer was up at the front throbbing like a heart... and people were moaning and groaning... and Lou was carrying on something awful... and I thought to myself... if God is looking down and has any sense of humour at all, He must be laughing his head off this very moment. Besides, He probably doesn't have any better idea of when the world is going to end than the rest of us. So I got up and left. Lou didn't even notice. It's a funny thing. Lou always thought it would come from so far away. The Almighty voice and the rain of locusts and blood. The moon turned dark and the stars gone wild. And all the time it was close by. We left the baby alone... we always did... slip over to the Vigil for an hour or so. No harm done. When I got home that night, the fire trucks were already there. It started in the basement spread. It was an old house. *(fighting back tears... holding the bottle up)* Lou says... she's always saying to me... well, Murray, you have the perfect excuse now.

from

Alphonse
by Wajdi Mouawad
translated by Shelley Tepperman

Premiered at the duMaurier Theatre, Toronto, 2001, directed by Lynda Hill and Alon Nashman. Script available from Playwrights Canada Press (English) and Leméac Éditeur (French).

• • •

"How Things Turned Out"

In the last scene, the narrator reveals himself.

ALPHONSE

I am Alphonse.

I'm the one people have said all kinds of things about from the beginning. I didn't mean to run away, or escape, I wasn't sad or unhappy and I loved my parents very much… in fact what happened is much simpler. I simply went in the wrong direction after taking the subway home after school. I didn't get off at the next station. Too tired. So I kept going, right to the end of the line. Everybody knows that in certain situations we don't know how to react. And when the invisible opens before us, it's terrifying. No one teaches us anything about the invisible. Not a thing. When we're children, no one tells us much. For example, when I was small, no one ever told me that the Earth is in a galaxy and that the stars are formed from a pile of stardust that binds together and forms a mass and grows and grows till it collapses onto itself and dying, creates enough energy to shine, sometimes for millions of years. No one ever said a word to me about that. But had I known, it seems to me that yes, it would have comforted me! Yes, it would have helped me sleep.

When Pierre-Paul-René entered the apartment, I don't know exactly what happened. But I can easily imagine. The front door. The hallway, my mother in the living room knitting, my father not talking, my sister sleeping (she must have been pretending) and my brother walking behind Pierre-Paul-René, all the way to my bed. Pierre-Paul-René lay down, he slept. That must be how things went; but what I'm sure of, is that no one

noticed a thing. No one could tell the different between Pierre-Paul-René and me. And no one will ever see the difference, because no one believes in Pierre-Paul-René. Everyone thinks that Pierre-Paul-René doesn't exist, people think that Pierre-Paul-René is a figment of my imagination! So they smile and look at each other and say: Oh, that Alphonse! Honestly! What an imagination! People only believe what they can see and touch! In fact, people don't want to believe anymore! They want to know. They don't believe that the earth is round, they know it. They don't believe that the sky is blue, they know it! And people have trapped what they know about me. What they knew about me. But the rest, everything else that's inside me, and around me, and that belongs to me, that part of me that's so small it has to be believed in, that part that's even more real than my flesh and blood can ever be, that part that their tired eyes will never be able to see, they haven't caught that part of me, it's still on the road as free as the colours of the night. That part of me is hidden, tucked away, buried; that's the part of me that truly exists. At least I want to believe that…
I want to believe it, so that life, which is just beginning for me, and death, which could strike me at any moment, will both be easier to accept, more joyful, and more beautiful.

from

Children
by Lawrence Jeffery

Premiered at Alberta Theatre Projects' playRites Festival, 1992, directed by
Bob White. Script available from Exile Editions.

• • •

BERTRAM

I was working for a roofing firm. We were working at a school. We were
doing the roof of the gymnasium. The inside of the gymnasium was
unfinished, there was still just sand on the floor.

Short pause.

When it happened I was inside the gym taking my coffee break and he
was up on the roof.… Before they put the tar and gravel topping on the
roof, before they even call the roofers in, they cut holes for the pipes—the
heating pipes and the water pipes and the ventilating ducts.… When they
finish with that they call the roofers. The first thing we do is cover the
whole roof with tar paper. There is this machine like a lawn mower tractor
goes all over the roof rolling out tar paper and tacking it down. Then some
insulation board goes over that, and then layers of hot tar and gravel.…
Well, this friend of mine was up on the roof like I said and I was down in
the gym… the gym was dark and the ceiling twenty feet above. I could hear
the tar paper machine going back and forth covering it.… He wasn't doing
that… I watched the spots of light go black after the machine crossed. It
was getting dark in the gym.… But I just watched. I didn't do anything.
I should have. I should have gone up and told them to cut the holes, that it
was dangerous, but I didn't.… So my friend's up on the roof getting ready
to do some tarring—first he's going to seal the edges of the roof with hot
tar.… The tar we used wasn't like pitch, it was oil sludge or something,
mean stuff.… It's heated in big vats by gas burners to 500ºF. It boils and
spits and there's blue smoke comes off it.… When it hits something it
sizzles, and the smoke get bluer and thicker.

Short pause.

So he's carrying these two buckets of tar across the roof to start sealing the edges.... He's walking across the roof when he steps on one of those covered up holes.... The paper busts through and he slips down like it was made for him. Stupid thing is he doesn't let go of the buckets. He holds on.... So he pulls the buckets down they catch on the roof and the tar covers him... I looked up when I heard the screaming... I've never heard such a sound.... In this beam of light from the roof was my friend... and he was falling, and screaming, and he was...

> *Short pause.*

He dropped into the sand in the circle of light from the hole in the roof. I ran to him. He's screaming. Making this sound and rolling over and over in the sand.

> *Brief pause.*

His eyes were sealed tight and his head and hands all black. I couldn't hold him, when I could I stuck to him and the smell of the tar and the smoke made me choke.... He was holding his hands up in front of his face and trying to open his mouth. Couldn't breathe—his mouth was sealed tight. So I held him as best I could and I... I stick my finger in his mouth and make an opening and I can see the flesh come away.

> *Brief pause.*

You know it's not so much the burns they worry about, not with tar. If you live as far as the hospital, it's not the burns, it's the chemicals they worry about. They can't get the tar off right away... so the chemicals have time to seep into the blood. These chemicals they're enough to kill you anyway.

> *Brief pause.*

Had more operations than I remember. I used to visit him but don't anymore. His wife goes to see him every day. She feeds him his dinner. You see he can't work his hands, there's no muscle left, nothing. They're stuff. Sticks.... So she comes to him every day and she feeds him because he can't do it himself.

from

Beating Heart Cadaver ✔
by Colleen Murphy

Premiered at the Canadian Stage Company, Toronto, produced by
Necessary Angel Theatre Company, 1998, directed by Richard Rose.
Script available from Playwrights Guild of Canada.

• • •

> *Leona and Danny lost their young daughter, Amelia, in a car*
> *accident. Danny's brother—rumoured to have ties to the IRA—*
> *comes to help. He tells Leona that his past is catching up with*
> *him.*

DEVLIN

I used to be in a band called The Constellations. Once we had a six-month
gig at the Constellation Hotel. The manager there was a Zodiac freak—he
thought that the Constellations playing at the Constellation held significant
astrological meaning so he offered us his personal psychic. Every week I'd
visit this Romanian with a tea cozy on her head and she'd feel up my aura,
"Oh, it's green today, Mr. Finn, and a very bright shade of green it is," then
she'd run her fingers up and down my life line and "My God, Mr. Finn, if
that isn't the longest life line I've yet encountered on a man, you'll live to
be one hundred at least." All these rosy predictions made me feel invincible
until one day she detected a shadow hovering round my aura and "Oh, Mr.
Finn, you're up to meeting a stranger in the near future." The next week
I asked her who was following me. "Oh, Mr. Finn, that'll be the darker side
of your nature trailing behind you, nothing to worry about." I joked that
maybe the stranger was lurking right outside her booth and might she put
up her psychic antennae and give me the lowdown on what they looked
like. She laughed. Now I wonder what shadow she'd seen hovering round
me and whether her dark side became attracted to my darker side or what
gobbley-gook transpired because the next morning she went missing. Four
days later a piece of her was mailed to the hotel… every day another chunk
arrived. Mr. Zodiac freaked out—during our breaks he'd scream about
Triangulum and Andromeda, yelling that the stars contained our death.
About three weeks after we finished the gig he was shot in the head and his

body stuffed into the truck of his car. I know who the stranger is, Leona...
and he's not very far behind me.

from

Bully
by Stephen Guy-McGrath and Steven Mayoff

Premiered at the Theatre Centre, Toronto, produced by Strange/Momentum Productions, 2003, directed by Ted Dykstra. Script available from Strange/Momentum Productions.

• • •

> Bully *is set in the imagination of Eugean Michael CARTER II, a man trapped in his childhood. At 12 he accidentally killed his schoolyard bully and has not been able to get past that moment in time. He is trying to explain to the audience what happened on that fateful day. By examining the past, he hopes to change his future.*

CARTER

I never walk or drive to school. I always fly. The orbit I follow to get to school is quite simple. Following a fairly straight trajectory up Military Road, I begin a low profile curve toward St. Bonaventure's Catholic School for boys of misadventure.

> *CARTER flies a simple repeated pattern.*

Down a block, over a block. Down a block, over a block. Down a block, over a block. Until I arrive at the gates of higher learning. I watch parents dropping off their children. A car pulls up. A child or two jumps out. The car drives away. Another car pulls up to fill the void left behind by the previous one. Nature abhors a vacuum. I have not arrived by automobile. I have flown. Flying has its sixes and sevens over walking or driving.

> *CARTER enters the classroom.*

In the school itself students whirl around. Sub-atomic particles. The positively charged Proton students try to find seats so they can continue to expand the universe that is their mind. The uncharged Neutron students do their best to maintain their momentum outside the learning curve. A marauding band of negativity. Father Carmine is the electromagnetic force that grinds all this activity to a halt. But the students remain restless.

Energy cannot be created or destroyed. There is nothing new under the sun. Everything that ever was always will be.

Three seats over, two seats back. Three seats over, two seats back. Three seats over, two seats back, to the chair where I sit. I always sit there. Everyone knows this is my seat and they always make sure not to sit there. It is the dead centre of the class. There is one last late arrival. Robert Glassco. The ultimate electron. We used to be friends but now he sneaks over the horizon like Nemesis the Death Star. He mere presence in the galaxy brings chaos. Every footstep reaps destruction. His gravity… is grave. When he is present all others are drawn to him and consumed by a black hole of ridicule. He gives higher learning a bad name.

> *Light shifts.*

Thank-you Father Carmine. A presentation on distillation. A controlled experiment. Distilling a benign liquid, Wink grape drink, into pure water. The life giver of the Universe. I am, as of yet, unable to create life. But I can give you water. The process is simple. All you need to do is heat a liquid, in this case Wink grape drink, to the point at which all of the H_2O transforms to a gas, approximately 98 degrees Celsius, and collect it. When you cool the gas, it will turn back into pure clean water. People have been using a similar method to make alcohol for centuries. Taking three hundred and fifty millilitres of Wink grape drink, I place it in a beaker with a cover that is attached to hose that leads to second covered beaker. The second beaker is placed off to the side and the first beaker is placed over the Bunsen burner to boil. With your patience, this should take approximately 2 minutes, 37 seconds and one half second.

> *CARTER looks at his watch. Light shifts.*

The faster one travels the slower time passes. The Twin Paradox. If you were to take a set of twin astronauts with exactly the same watches. Leave one on earth and send the other travelling around the universe on a spaceship that flies very near the speed of light. When she returned after a number of years her watch will have passed a few minutes and she will not have aged at all. And the astronaut that was left behind? Will be old and haggard. OH!… and her watch will need a new battery.

If our space travelling astronaut were to fall into a black hole just before her watch turned to midnight, it never would. The closer she got to the event horizon the slower her watch would go. The second hand would slow to the point that the last few seconds before midnight would take hours or days to pass. But the very last second. The very last second would never pass. She would be trapped forever in that moment of space-time.

> *CARTER looks at his watch. Light shifts.*

Sorry Father Carmine. As the Bunsen burner heats the three hundred and fifty milliliters of Wink grape drink, it will begin to boil, and the H_2O will evaporate and steam will travel up the hose. Once out of the direct heat of the Bunsen burner, the steam will begin to cool and change back into water. Pure H_2O dripping into the second beaker.

Unfortunately I was working with a closed pressurized system. I covered both beakers. There was nowhere for the steam to go. Nature abhors a vacuum!

It won't be long now at all until the distillation demonstration commences, please, just bear with me Father.

Suddenly the pressure became too much for the little beaker to bear. There was a big bang as the top of the first covered beaker burst off and flew into the front row of students, dragging the hose and the second covered beaker with it. The students dove from their stools to safety underneath the lab stations. The second beaker smashed, gracefully sending shards of glass spinning out in all directions. A supernova!

Father Carmine took refuge in the closet. The first beaker was left balancing over the still-flaming Bunsen burner with the Wink grape drink now boiling out of control.

Time slowed and chaos ensued as I tried to explain through strict scientific process what had happened. "The pressure of the beakers was too much. Ah, it's not possible to do this experiment at sea level." "It broke!"

from

Toronto at Dreamer's Rock
by Drew Hayden Taylor

Premiered at the Sheshegwaning Reserve, Manitoulin Island, 1989, directed by Larry Lewis. Script available from Fifth House Publishers.

• • •

> Toronto at Dreamer's Rock *is the story of three Ojibway boys,*
> *from different times in history, meeting at the top of a sacred*
> *rock.*

RUSTY

Oh yeah? Look at you. I have no idea what kind of outfit that is but it don't look like you're too bad off. And judging by the way you talk and the things you've said, you're doing great in school and you know a lot of things. Keesic here only has to worry about hunting enough to eat. They didn't have complicated problems back then. At least you both have your own worlds to fit in and return to. I'm stuck smack-dab in the middle of a family war, between one uncle that's called "Closer" because they say he's closed every bar in Ontario, and my other, Uncle Stan, who is basically a powwow Indian, I never know what's going on. Sometimes I don't know if I should go into a sweatlodge or a liquor store. Sometimes they tear me apart. I don't fit in. Like tonight. It's Saturday and what am I doing? Standing on a rock, out in the middle of the woods, talking to two people who probably don't exist. How's that for a social life? Instead of looking at the two of you, I should be out with some hot babe.

from

The Weekend Healer
by Bryden MacDonald

Premiered at the Factory Theatre, Toronto, 1994, directed by Annie Kidder.
Script available from Talonbooks.

• • •

CURTIS

You try bein sixteen today!
You just try bein sixteen today.
I dare ya—for five minutes.
You try bein sixteen
bein big an stupid and nowhere.
You try bein sixteen watchin me watch you fuck up:
that goof loves his car more than he loves you—always did.
He still thinks he's gonna make the NHL for crissake
and the only thing bigger
than his swelled friggin head is his gut.
If he don't like it—he hits it:
fuckin Fred Flintstone.
But don't listen ta me—
I'm just sixteen.
Jesus Christ ma—
who's raisin who here?
What am I gonna end up like?
What am I gonna end up like huh?
You try bein sixteen.
You just try bein sixteen
in a world run by arseholes
that are older than your dead fuckin grandfather.
You try bein sixteen
dealin with those arseholes
and their fuckin Noah's Ark rocket ships ta nowhere.
Ta where? The moon? Mars?
Inta the fuckin sky!
Who cares?

I don't.
Why don't they just go?
Stop talking about it an go!
Get! Leave!
Leave us alone. Leave me alone.
I'm not afraid ta be left behind.
I wanna be left behind
but only if those fuckers go.
But they won't. No.
They just sit around talkin about it
spendin money that could be feedin people
on their bullshit rockets!
But who's gonna listen ta me?
I'm just one a the stupid kids
that gotta live in their stupider world
if there's anything left in this fuckin world
by the time they get done with it.
Why don't they just leave us alone?
I don't want no part
of condo-fuckin-miniums on the moon.

>   *He catches his breath.*

Fuck.

>   *A long awkward silence.*

from

Jason
by Betty Jane Wylie

Premiered at Under the Umbrella, Toronto, directed by Andrew Chown.
Script available from Playwrights Guild of Canada.

• • •

> *JASON is a "high-functioning" retarded young man who is
> being interviewed by a panel of judges, residents of a co-op
> housing complex that is considering allowing him and a buddy
> to live in one of the apartments. Though he started out neat
> enough, he is dishevelled as he tries very hard to answer the
> sometimes disconcerting questions he is asked. The entire play
> is a monologue as Jason answers these questions. At one point
> he looks at a mirror and approaches it. The lights change subtly
> and he speaks:*

JASON

Is this, is this a two-way mirror? Is there someone on the other side
watching me?

> *It's a free-standing mirror-frame. He walks around, looks at the
> other side.*

No, it isn't. I know about two-way mirrors because when they ask you
questions and stuff sometimes they want you too sometimes. Basically
someone's always watching you.

> *He comes back, looks at himself in the mirror. He straightens,
> smoothes his hair, adjusts his tie, tucks in his shirt tail. Suddenly
> he looks much less… odd. He speaks. We should be able to see
> his face.*

> *This is his alter ego speaking—perhaps what he would sound
> like if he were normal.*

Mirrors are disconcerting at best. You see before you a mentally challenged
young man and you proceed to make all kinds of assumptions. You all treat
me as though you had a right to my privacy. Some people's information is

private. All my information belongs to anyone who cares to ask, but they don't listen much, not closely. Oddly enough, I don't mind all the questions. I keep hoping someone will listen to me, so I don't complain. You have the right to my personal information—you *think* you have the right—and since you get it, I have to surmise that you do have the right, to ask my about my innermost desires, my plans, hopes, fears for the future, my sex life, my libido, my aches and pains, my anger, my fear, my affections, my gratitude and my obligations, my fantasies and expectations—mine, and those imposed on me.

> *Pause.*

But I can't ask you those things. If I asked you I would be considered nosy, impertinent and invasive of your privacy.

> *He checks the mirror again.*

It would be so much easier for you if I *looked* acceptable. I can see that. I see it all the time. It's hard for people to accept what they don't understand. You, for example, you are good people, kind enough, well-meaning, but you'd really like to know what you're letting yourself in for if you let people like Bud and me into the co-op. You're wondering whether I'll pee on the grass or put condoms in the dryer. You're fearful for your two-year-olds and protective of your teenage daughters. A neat, presentable young man just has to be safer than a slack-jawed, shuffling, smiling dummy, doesn't he? Isn't that what you're thinking? So you have questions that you wouldn't think of insulting a more intelligent-looking person with.

Go ahead and ask your questions. Consult your file. I see you have a file on Jason Bowman. There is no real Jason, just the paper one. There is a schedule for Jason Bowman. The schedule puts Jason on the set in the spotlight at a specific moment in time—this one. When the light goes out, Jason will cease to exist. Jason, after all, is not really human.

Jason is a retard.

from

Soulless
by Aaron Bushkowsky

Premiered at Rumble Theatre, Vancouver, 2004, directed by
Norman Armour. Script available from the playwright at
aaronbushkowsky@telus.net.

• • •

> *DARREN is a lawyer who has been in the business for many*
> *years. He's working with Bob, a developer who's had a woman*
> *from Social Housing threatening to shut down the new condo*
> *development. Here, DARREN is in Bob's office. Light knifes*
> *through the slats in the blinds. Bob is in the dark nearby*
> *listening. DARREN paces.*

DARREN

So, a woman is bothering you at work? She comes and goes as she pleases.
She has no respect for your privacy or your personal space. She threatens to
stop the development. Stop the development? Stop the development? Well,
I think we have a case for harassment, don't you? I can make this work,
don't you worry. It doesn't matter how huge your company is, or how
wealthy you are. I've defended some of the biggest banks in business and if
you knew how much they screwed you, you wouldn't want them to win.
Check your statement lately? Who does, right? A buck here, a buck there.
Whatever. As long as it's convenient. Anyway, the long story short, I've
never lost a case because I never give people a choice between good or bad.
Not about that. It's about the thin line between. A truth all of its own. And
that, my friend, is what we can get away with. Think about Woody Allen,
mid-career Woody, not washed up weirdo Woody doing old guy comedy
with young nubile women one-third his age. Jesus. *(beat)* "Crimes and
Misdemeanors"… God, that was so full… what you can get away with.
And truth and there are many paths to the truth or away from it. And
really, that's the cool thing about being a lawyer. We're actually filmmakers.
We just paint a picture… we dabble in the grey areas: we show how people
can be fragile and confused, and let's say, disconnected. We all are. Come
on, life is difficult, right? A man sits in his empty kitchen, a bare lightbulb

over his head. He is broken, sobbing… things are piling up, bills, bills, bills. He hasn't slept in days. He's about to lose his job and he is *exactly* like us. A shell of a man. Crumbling into dust. Who could blame him?

(beat) I love movies. If I wasn't a lawyer I'd be making movies. Good movies always have moral dilemmas. Good people do bad things, that sorta element. But things are changing, right? Sometimes it pisses me off. Didn't movies used to be about "do I trust this person?" then suddenly they changed to "do I trust what's going on?" and now they're "do I trust *me*, my own perceptions?" What happened? *(beat)* Even in our dreams we've become paranoid narcissists, haven't we?

So, where does that leave us?

Well, I want you to notice, I didn't say "enlightenment." I would never say that. Never. More than ever it's just about how we live and what we do, not why. And that's exactly why I practice law.

from

House
by Daniel MacIvor

Premiered at the Factory Theatre, Toronto, produced by Da Da Kamera in association with Factory Theatre, 1992, directed by Daniel Brooks. Script available from Playwrights Canada Press.

• • •

> *VICTOR is a man pushed to the edge of his world, teetering on the edge of reality and struggling not to slip.*

VICTOR

I was gonna be an engineer. But I'm not.

I was gonna be an engineer.

I was gonna be an engineer for two reasons. First reason of why I wanted to be an engineer was because engineers are the guys who figure out how to build things so they don't fall down. Figure out how to build the floor so the ceiling won't cave in, figure out how to build the ceiling so the walls won't bend. Now that is useful information, especially if you've ever had anything fall on you.

The second reason why I wanted to be an engineer was because THEY'RE SO FUNNY! Oh yeah, engineers are the guys who on April Fool's put a Volkswagen on the roof of the cafeteria or fill the Dean's office with liquid insulation. NOW THAT'S FUNNY! But it is to be *respected* because it's not a joke. It's not. Any idiot can tell a joke, I could tell a joke, but it's not a joke, it's a… prank! Ah! And a prank! is to be *respected* because it involves COMRADERY! Ah! Comradery! I never had any comradery. Comradery was something I saw twenty-five yards away in a field with a bunch of guys and a ball. I never had any comradery. (If we had violins we'd play them.) You know. Comradery, when you're a kid and you're gonna put a frog in a paper bag and set it on fire and throw it on somebody's doorstep, you gotta figure out whose doorstep, who's gonna catch the frog, who's not scared of frogs, who's gonna put the frog in the bag, who's not scared of warts, who's gonna set the bag on fire, who's not scared of getting burnt. You know comradery. And engineers are the most comraderistic people in the whole world and I always imagined that when they'd be doing their prank, they'd all be up in some office where they broke in late at night with a skeleton key and they'd be putting the photocopier in the water cooler then when they were finished they'd come down into the street being all quiet and happy and proud of their prank and the sun would just be coming up and they'd be saying beautiful poetic things to one another like:

"See ya tomorrow."

"Call ya Friday."

"Wanna go for breakfast?"

And that might not sound like poetry but it does if you never heard it and I never did.

I was gonna be an engineer but I'm not.

from

Here Lies Henry
by Daniel MacIvor and Daniel Brooks

Premiered at the Six Stages Festival at Buddies in Bad Times Theatre, Toronto, 1995, directed and dramaturged by Daniel Brooks. Script available from Playwrights Canada Press.

• • •

> *HENRY is a liar who is trying to tell the audience something they don't already know.*

HENRY

You know… I have a feeling. And I have a feeling that: we're a lot alike. It's simple… it's obvious… it's just the nature of existence. 1, 2, 3.

One, you're born.

Two, you assume… yes… a series of—I don't know—experiences.

Three, you die.

One, you're born: dark passage into a bright room.

Two, you assume… yes… a series of—I don't know—experiences:

You learn to walk.

You learn to talk.

You have your first day of school.

You get a dog, or a cat, or a gerbil, or a turtle; it runs away or dies.

You can't wait for Christmas.

You collect things: matchbooks, Boy Scout badges, cardboard.

You enter puberty and spend two fabulous years in your bedroom with James Taylor…. Or Carly Simon or whatever the case may be.

You get your driver's license.

You leave home.

You never write, but you call!

You think about going to college and you don't, or you do.

You lose your ideals and drift aimlessly toward the void.

Until *(drum roll)* you meet your love in a laundromat or a party. You take that wonderful walk you make that perfect promise; or *(drum roll)* you convince yourself that some people just weren't meant to couple.

But either way you seize the day, you change your mind, you make a plan, you resolve to stop, to start, to seize the day to change your mind to make a plan. You, in short, experience. Three, you die:

Bright passage into a dark room.

Dark passage into a bright room, experience experience experience, bright passage into a dark room. Dark passage into a bright room, bright passage into a dark room, dark passage into a bright room, bright passage into a dark room, bright into a dark, dark into a bright into a dark into bright into dark into bright. Shoom!

And that's the hook and here's a catch and the catch of the day is sole. And the bone that runs down the middle, from which grows the fillet, the spine of the soul, is Hope.

And of course there's always hope.

Of course there's always hope!

Of course, there's always hope.

Of course, there's always hope?

And of course you have hope.

But that is where we differ.

from

Blood
by Tom Walmsley

Premiered at the Factory Theatre, Toronto, 1995, directed by David Ferry.
Script available from Scirocco Drama.

· · ·

CHRIS explains how twelve-step programs actually work.

CHRIS

I used to pray every night that you'd find the program, you'd come to
meetings. Okay, sure, I can see where you'd have problems. We all do. The
first time you see the signs at the front of the room, the slogans, it's bad
news. There's these clichés, one day at a time, keep it simple, easy does it.
What the fuck am I doing here? It's easy to think you're too smart for it.
But let me tell you, you think they're clichés, but let me tell you. *(pause)*
Well, they are clichés. That's a fact. I had a sponsor, I got rid of him,
I haven't had one in years, but this guy said, there's a reason clichés have
become clichés. Right? He's saying they're true, they've lasted through
time, that's how they became clichés. I felt better. And then, all of a sudden,
I didn't feel better anymore. They've been around a long time, it means
fuck all. Santa Claus has been around a long time. Neckties have been
around a long time, and there is nothing more useless than a fucking
necktie. Clichés, you believe them, you become one. A cliché is, it's like
a necktie. It's the necktie you hang yourself with in your cell. God damn it,
I'm writing that down. I can never think of those things at the time. Listen.
The thing is, you can stop using drugs. It'll work. It shouldn't work, but it
does. Because of God.

from

Theatre of the Film Noir
by George F. Walker

Premiered at the Factory Theatre, Toronto, 1981, directed by George F. Walker. Script available from Talonbooks.

• • •

BERNARD

I've lost it. Jesus Christ, come help me. I've lost it.

> *He mumbles, groans, whines. Suddenly something on the ground catches his eye.*

What's that?

> *He whines, groans, whimpers. He crawls quickly along the ground. Stops. Picks up a small coin. Sighs, giggles.*

Where have you been. I was sick with worry. Now go back where you belong. *(puts the coin in his pocket)* And never try to escape again. Is my life cheap to you.

> *There is an open grave a few feet away from him. A wooden casket on the ground beside it. He walks over to it. Addresses the casket.*

I found it. I'll be all right now. *(sits on the casket, lights a cigarette)* I know you'd be laughing. And I know what you'd be saying. "Bernard, you're a superstitious fool." *(takes a drag on the cigarette)* Ah well, what of it. I found that coin the day the Nazis invaded. God whispered strangely in my ear. Here's a little two-headed coin for you, Bernard. A little token of my affection that will see you through the dark times ahead. It was one of those rare moments when God chose subtlety instead of outright terror. Nevertheless the point was well taken and I have kept this with me at all times. I know you'd be laughing, Jean. But I have been shot at with pistols, rifles, machine guns and cannons and I am still alive. True, I am a coward. But I am alive. *(crushes his cigarette, stands)* And you are dead. You should have let God whisper in your ear. You should have let him give you a coin. You should have learned to run and hide like me.

He opens the casket, takes out a bottle of wine, takes a long drink, puts the bottle back in the casket, closes the lid.

from

Lion in the Streets
by Judith Thompson

Premiered at the duMaurier Theatre, Toronto, 1990, directed by Judith
Thompson. Script available from Playwrights Canada Press.

• • •

> *FATHER HAYES describes the horror he feels at the death of*
> *a child he sees as inevitable.*

FATHER HAYES

Because… of what was to happen, in the water: oh OH when the day
arrived, when the picnic came round, in July, that Canada Day picnic?
I had a bad feeling, I had… a very bad feeling indeed. We all piled out of
the cars: families, priests, nuns, altar boys, piled out and lugged all those
picnic baskets to tables under trees. The grownups all fussed with food and
drink while the kids, all of your children, ran ran in your white bare feet to
the water, throwing stones and balls, and a warning sound a terrible, the
sound of deep nausea filled my ears and I looked up and saw you, dancing
on the water, and I saw a red circle, a red, almost electric circle, dazzling
round and round like waves, spinning round your head and body.
I thought watch, watch that boy, on this day he will surely drown, he
will. David, *I knew that you would die.* All because of the chicken. The
twenty-nine-pound chicken brought there by Mrs. Henry, grown on her
brother's farm, everyone had talked and talked about that chicken, who
would carve that chicken, Mrs. Henry took it out you skipped along the
shore, she laid it on the table, "FATHER HAYES, YOU GO AHEAD AND
CARVE, AND DON'T MAKE A MESS OF IT OR YOU WON'T SEE ME
AT MASS NEXT SUNDAY." Everyone laughed, the men, the men drinking
beer, watching me, sure they're thinking, "Watch him carve like a woman,"
most men hate priests, you know this is a fact, I could see them thinking
cruel thoughts under hooded eyes and practised grins; my sin was the sin
of pride! The sin of pride David, I started to carve, didn't want to look up,
lest I wreck the bird. You see at that moment the chicken was worth more,
indeed worth more… than your LIFE, David I SHUT OUT the warning
voice and I—carved. I carved and carved and ran into trouble, real trouble

I remember thinking, "Damn how does any person do it, it's a terrible job," people behave as if it's nothing, but it's terrible, I kept at it, I wouldn't give up, I wouldn't look up till I'd finished, and I finished carving, and I had made a massacre. The men turned away the women... murmured comfort, and before I looked up I had a hope, a hard hope, that you were still skipping on the rocks and shouting insults to your pals all hands reached for chicken and bread, potato salad, chocolate cake I looked I looked up and your hand from the sea, your hand, far away, was reaching, reaching for me far away... oh no! I ran, and tripped, fell on my face ran again, I couldn't not speak ran to the water and shouted as loud as I could but my voice was so tiny; I saw your hand, ran to the fisherman close, he wasn't home his fat daughter and I, in the skiff, not enough wind no wind, paddling paddling, you a small spot nothing then nothing the sun burns our faces our red red faces.

from

Half Life
by John Mighton

Premiered at the Tarragon Theatre, Toronto, co-produced by Necessary
Angel Theatre, 2005, directed by Daniel Brooks. Script available from
Playwrights Canada Press.

• • •

DONALD

This summer, at the cottage, I was aware that I was having fun, but my
enjoyment was always overshadowed by so many concerns—worries about
the future, about my daughter Nina, my work, even worries about the
way our activities were affecting the lake—there were huge boathouses
springing up everywhere—all part of the relentless development of the
north. But looking back, a few weeks later, I cried—I felt the pure joy of
watching Nina jump into the water over and over. I remember the way she
and her friends named every dive—"The pencil." "The chair." "The dead
man."—even though every dive was essentially the same, but the way they
laughed, the way they shouted out the names, the anticipation… it was so
simple… they will never be happier—I cried for that, because it was so
simple and so hard to reproduce—because it would never happen again….
People should be put to death at age ten…. What purpose does growing old
serve?

from

Stone and Ashes
by Daniel Danis
translated by Linda Gaboriau

Premiered at the Factory Theatre, Toronto, 1994, directed by Jackie Maxwell.

• • •

NOODLE

Every time we got carried away, the five of us
I'd let out a cry from deep down inside
like when you call a moose
to get the hate out of me.

Then I'd yell:
"Gulka. Attack."
With the legs of a stag
I could hear him running
along the path of my veins.
From his wolverine jaws
came a terrifying roar.
Gulka escaped through my eyes.
He was taking my place.
I was become stronger, taller
a kind of angry god.
I was becoming Gulka.

During the Gulf War
we saw soldiers talking on TV.
Almost my age
they were in the desert
and I was sitting there doing nothing
drinking my cold beer.
They were outta their minds
believing they were invincible.

I saw Shirley
sitting on the flowered rug.
I was thinking about Gulka
staring at the foam on my beer.
Except for Grandad
no one knew about him.
An animal inside me
my forest burned to the ground
a ruined man.
Nothing left.

My mother asked me:
"What are you going to do with your life, Neal?
You're twenty-nine years old.
If you're not satisfied with your jobs
you could go back to school.
Go on to university."

"Shit, Ma
Go back to school
to get some dumb diploma
and then end up with the same goddamn joe jobs."

"I don't know, take a trip
have fun, buy a house,
set up housekeeping with someone.
Have some kids."

"No job in the offing,
no wife in sight
nothing clear
shit, Ma
I won't come back here
if you keep bugging me about that."

"Let's change the subject, it's your life
do what you want with it."

"Not what I want, what I can."

"You want some more stew, Neal?"

"Don't mind if I do, Ma, it's so good."

"I just wish you had one little dream.
Anyway."

       Beat.

"Ma, I already told you.
Dreams are
for people who believe in God
doesn't matter which one.
Any god.
A dream for hope.
Dreams are
for people who imagine some paradise exists.
My generation
we try to get by on our own.
With no gods anywhere.
With no jobs anywhere.

We see life the way it is.
We don't pretty it up.
We were born at the wrong time.
There are no right times.
Your stew is great, Ma.
That's my idea of happiness
having supper at my mother's house
two or three times a week."

A man at the end of his rope
my forest is empty
a starving animal.
I'm looking for a dream
a dream I could invent for myself
once and for all.
But I can't see anything.
My forest is dead.
Gulka is big and fat.

from

Born Ready
by Joseph Jomo Pierre

Premiered at Theatre Passe Muraille, Toronto, co-produced by Obsidian
Theatre Company and Theatre Passe Muraille, 2005. Script available from
Playwrights Canada Press.

• • •

> BLACKMAN *details his early beginnings and memories,*
> *exposing the experiences that helped to mold him.*

BLACKMAN

I'm from two large buildings, and four small ones. I'm from a small one-
bedroom that neva faced the sun. We had a patch of grass in the middle.
The grass was neva green. Matter of fact by mid-summer that grass was just
dirt. When I was little, that patch of grass is where everything went down.
I'd see the kids a little bigger than me playing stickball in the day. And the
older folks huddle in the courts at night. Sometimes someone would walk
across to the huddle, and they would laugh and give dap *(type of greeting*
eg. knocking of fists). And then the man would walk away. That's how they
did it, that's how the deals went down. A little cream *(money)* for the green
(weed).

Moms was Trinidadian. A real beautiful woman. She neva took shit. My
pops couldn't get away with shit around her. My mother was the type of
woman that would skin a nigga's dick if she got crossed. *(laughs)* I figure
pops enjoyed having skin on his cock, he ain't get on her wrong side too
often. Don't think I eva seen him hit her. Don't get me wrong, that man
was tough. He spoke with one of those heavy tongues. Like his word was
bond. I seen my old man out on that patch of grass some nights. He be part
of the huddle. Moms always had something on her mind. I was a little fuck,
but I knew that she wasn't right. There was always something eating at her.

Seven years old when my father died. *(pause)* His body face down in that
patch of grass.

Seven when whatever that was wrong with my mother killed her.

So basically my aunt raised me. But her building was a nightmare. I mean if Moms had hard times, my aunt had it worst. Sleeping in there was hell. First off, I had to share a room with my cousin. She was cool, but I useta have these real fuckin intense nightmares, and I always felt strange being weirded out in front of her. Then there was those fuckin demons. *(starts tapping his hands on the floor)* you hear that *(taps)* shhh, when the light go out, shhh, you hear them. *(He taps more. It sounds like little footsteps.)* Those fucks running ova your head. *(taps)* Back and forth like they fighting a damn war. Sounds like there is a million of them. Like any moment the ceiling will bust and they'll drop all ova my face. Then the walls start. *(taps)* Just running like it's their fucking house. Like who the fuck was I, it's their crib. *(makes sound with his mouth)* Then I hear it. *(makes sound again)* Right under my bed. Like inches below my pillow I hear the shits talking to each other. *(makes sound)* And I hear them running… I'll come straight with you. I had some bitch in me when I was small. I useta go into my cousin's bed. She useta wrap her arms around me until I fell asleep. Wasn't shit sexual, you know. It was all, it was all just needing to feel safe.

from

Wild Abandon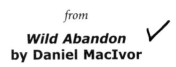
by Daniel MacIvor

Premiered at Theatre Passe Muraille, Toronto, produced by Sword Theatre in association with Theatre Passe Muraille, 1988, directed by Vinetta Strombergs. Script available from Playwrights Canada Press.

• • •

STEVE

I go to this diner.

Not a rest-o-rant I hate rest-o-rants I never go to rest-o-rants I only go to diners. And I only go to diners that have all-day breakfasts because who the hell are they to tell me when I should eat breakfast? Who the hell are they to tell me when I should get out of bed? This particular breakfast this particular day was three, four o'clock. Sausages, hash browns, WHITE toast, BLACK coffee and eggs over EASY! Very easy, so you can still taste the rawness in the yolk; so you can almost… taste… that… chicken.

Sometimes jam sometimes not depends on the day this day no. So I'm sitting there looking out the window thinking about how when trees are dead and the leaves are gone you can see so much more of the world and this woman four, four and a half feet away left side starts talking to her friend in this pretty loud voice about this trip she took to Mexico.

"There were so many Gringos."

Yeah. I'm serious. Gringos. That's what she said.

And then? Every time the guy brings something over to the table she goes "Gracias!"

Gracias like she took one trip there and she turns into fucking Mexico. But that be okay, but that be okay until she starts talking about being on this bus with all these "Men" and she says "Men" like it's some kind of disease or a bad drug. "Men."

And what am I? I'm a man. I'm a man sitting right there. She'd be looking right at me if she'd just turn her head this much. She practically is staring at me without even moving her eyes at all. I'm right there!

Then! Out of nowhere, she's telling her friend about the Grand Canyon. The fucking Grand Canyon's not in Mexico!

What am I supposed to think right?

THEN! Fuck…. Then she's describing this dream she had where all these "Men" are growing out of the walls of her apartment. All these "Men." So I was pretty fed up right—

And not because she's a woman, don't think that okay, I got nothing against women. Persons I got something against. And this woman here it was just her Person-Ality that was pissing me off… and how she was saying all this shit just so somebody would hear her. I'm sitting right there!

So.

So I lean over and I say: "Excuse me. Why don't you go get some help!" Yeah I did.

No I didn't.

I didn't say that. What I said was: "If you want to sleep with me why don't you just say so?"

No I didn't.

I didn't say nothing.

>   *Pause.*

But you know what I did do though?

I got up, and I changed my seat!

That's almost as good as saying something.

And I never went back to that diner either.

Not because of her… but because they got my fucking eggs wrong!

from

Napalm the Magnificent: Dancing With the Dark
by David S. Craig

Premiered at Roseneath Theatre, Toronto, 1996, directed by Richard Greenblatt. Script available from Playwrights Guild of Canada.

• • •

A theatre critic explains his motives.

CRITIC

Well you see… *(puffs)* I'm a theatre critic. I've seen a thousand plays in the past three years and I've only liked the first act of one. It was a production of *The Tempest*. Prospero made his entrance crawling out of the mud. English director. God they know Shakespeare… sometimes. The thing is, I don't know why I keep going. Obviously, I don't enjoy it. I much prefer going to movies. A good movie is great, a bad movie is funny. A good play is rare, a bad play leaves me depressed for weeks. I just can't keep opening myself up like that and still be critical. That's why I developed a system. First, I always read the press release and make up my mind before I go. That way I have an opinion in case I arrive late, or leave early or just drift off in the middle, which, let's face it, happens. Then, I always dismiss the content. If the issue is evident, I say the playwright has gone too far. If it isn't, I say the playwright hasn't gone far enough. It saves me grappling with issues I don't understand. After all, I can only write from experience and my experience is seeing six to eight plays a week. What do I like? *(long pause)* Well, I suppose I like being a bitch. Deciding what's good and bad. Being the public judge of the cultural agenda. Sleeping in every morning, I don't know. What I'd really like to do is write a cheap sex thriller and use a pseudonym. But who has time to do what they really want. Naturally, in my frame of mind, being critical is a lot easier than being positive. In fact, when I see people at the theatre enjoying themselves I just assume they're friends of the actors, or from out of town. And then a bad review usually gets a better headline, which means a better place in the entertainment section, but I'm not influenced by those considerations. I just don't really like theatre anymore. In fact, I can't remember why I ever did.

Index by Author

Index by Title

Publisher/Theatre Contact Information

Dundurn Press
3 Church St. Suite 500
Toronto, ON M5E 1M2
Phone: (416) 214-5544
Fax: (416) 214-5556
www.dundurn.com
info@dundurn.com

Exile Editions
20 Dale Ave.
Toronto, ON M4W 1K4
Phone: (416) 922-8221
Fax: (416) 922-8221
www.exileeditions.com
books@exileeditions.com

Fifth House Publishers
1800 – 4th St. SW, #1511
Calgary, AB T2S 2S5
Phone: 1 (800) 387-9776
Fax: (403) 571-5235
www.fitzhenry.ca/fifthhouse.aspx
godwit@fitzhenry.ca

Great North Artists Management
350 Dupont St.
Toronto, ON M5R 1V9
Phone: (416) 925-2051
Fax: (416) 925-3904
renazimmerman@gnaminc.com

Ground Zero Theatre
144, 517 – 10th Avenue S.W.
Calgary, AB T2R 0A8
Phone: (403) 202-2520
Fax: (403) 230-5510
www.groundzerotheatre.ca
info@groundzerotheatre.ca

House of Anansi Press
110 Spadina Ave., #801
Toronto, ON M5V 2K4
Phone: (416) 363-4343
Fax: (416) 363-1017
www.anansi.ca
info@anansi.ca

Leméac Éditeur
4609 rue Iberville, 3e étage
Montreal, PQ H2H 2L9
Phone: (514) 524-5558
Fax: (514) 524-3145
lemeac@lemeac.com

NeWest Press
201, 8540 – 109 Street
Edmonton, AB T6G 1E6
Phone: 1 (866) 796-5473
Fax: (780) 433-3179
www.newestpress.com
orders@newestpress.com